Healing the World

Healing the World

A Primer About the World and How We Must Fix it for Our Children

by
David E. Christensen

Foreword by Sheila Simon

iUniverse, Inc.
New York Lincoln Shanghai

Healing the World
A Primer About the World and How We Must Fix it for Our Children

iUniverse books may be ordered through booksellers or by contacting:

iUniverse
2021 Pine Lake Road, Suite 100
Lincoln, NE 68512
www.iuniverse.com
1-800-Authors (1-800-288-4677)

ISBN-13: 978-0-595-36386-5 (pbk)
ISBN-13: 978-0-595-80823-6 (ebk)
ISBN-10: 0-595-36386-5 (pbk)
ISBN-10: 0-595-80823-9 (ebk)

Printed in the United States of America

NOTE: The composite satellite photo on the cover was taken as the Earth was turning toward the east. We see twilight overtaking West Africa, the Iberian Peninsula (Spain and Portugal), the western edge of France, the British Isles and the southern part and west coast of Norway, with evening "lights coming on" in the darkened areas to the east.

On the one hand it shows natural features: ice-covered Greenland in the upper left corner, Iceland, the Sahara, ocean depths, the mid-Atlantic ridge and continental shelf. And on the other hand, the scattered "lights" across Europe, Russia and West Africa south of the Sahara (with oil field flares off Nigeria's coast) are evidence of major impacts we humans are having on our Earth home.

Credit for the cover photo goes to NASA's Earth Observatory team for developing the imagery: <http://earthobservatory.nasa.gov/>.

CONTENTS

ACKNOWLEDGEMENTS

Following up my suggestions to Paul Simon in the fall of 2003, and my sharing thoughts with my family and others about a "follow up book" to Paul's "Healing America", a number of individuals encouraged me to take up writing a book about "Healing the World". Among the earliest encouragers were my four children, Danley, Alan, Karen and Shari, and their families. There were several intensive months as the manuscript went through two drafts before I let others take a look. I instructed those who received copies to review not to hold back from their criticism and surely not to read it as something written by their Dad or a friend.

For their suggestions, my thanks goes to two Alan Christensens (my brother and my son), my son Danley, daughters Karen and Shari, my sister Dorothy, and the following friends: Kris Juul, David Gobert, Bill Sasso, Bob Lembcke and Sheila Simon. I have used most of their suggestions, as well as those from the iUniverse publishers, in a final revision. All of them will note that this final manuscript is different from the one they had critiqued.

Inasmuch as Paul Simon's book, Healing America, was the inspiration for my book, I thought it appropriate for his daughter Sheila to write a Foreword. So my special thanks also to Sheila Simon, Paul Simon's very busy daughter, for the Foreword she so kindly wrote. She is a law professor at Southern Illinois University Carbondale, a member of the Carbondale City Council, and a member of the Illinois Arts Council.

FOREWORD

My father, Paul Simon, had great respect for Dave Christensen. Dad valued Dave's opinions enough to ask Dave for feedback on one of Dad's last books. After reading this book I understand Dad's appreciation for Dave.

Dave's book is based in part on Dad's work, but they shared more than ideas. Dad and Dave have written in similar styles, full of problems, plans and dreams. They shared an optimistic enthusiasm for what people, working together, can accomplish. They also shared an urgency, a sense that talking and writing are not enough.

I hope you will enjoy this book as I have. Read it; share it; and act on it!

Sheila Simon
July 14, 2005

HEALING THE WORLD

A Primer About the World and How We Must Fix It for Our Children

INTRODUCTION

In an important way Former United States Senator Paul Simon (from Illinois) is responsible for this book. His book, <u>Healing America</u> was published in August 2003. I had been privileged to read an early draft and make a few suggestions. After its publication I suggested to Paul, since America cannot be healed in isolation from the rest of the world, he ought to write a sequel, "Healing the World". His comment was that it was an interesting idea but he had other priorities on his agenda at that time.

I reread <u>Healing America</u> and realized many of his ideas and examples did address directly a "Healing the World" theme. I thought he might simply develop a book about "Healing the World" by pulling these together and adding to them. I also mentioned this idea to him, but, tragically, he died suddenly a few weeks later in December 2003 and those conversations and thoughts came to naught.

I felt strongly that "Healing the World" had to be written. I realized, being a retired geographer with a keen interest in the well-being of the world and being a long-term optimist, that many of my concerns and thoughts and writings over the years carried a "healing the world" theme. I also have believed for decades that Limited World Government is essential to any solution. With that focus this book took shape over many months during 2004 and early 2005.

This book is dedicated to Paul and to my wife, Carol, who died two months before Paul. Over the fifty seven years of our marriage Carol and I had many conversations about the concerns and ideas that are in this book. Carol and I traveled, taught, and lectured in eighteen countries from 1949 to 1999, and in doing so we observed and learned much about our Earth and our friendly and helpful neighbors on this planet. Carol also was an excellent editor and sounding board for everything I thought and wrote, from thesis to dissertation to professional articles and "letters to the editor", so I miss her very much in this endeavor.

In this book I have quoted from Paul's <u>Healing America</u> and his other books several times, and I have included quotes from dozens of others. I have paid particular attention to key problems that focus on our country and the world as I see it. As "citizens of the world" we must work together toward a world in peace that will not leave for our children the many problems with which we struggle today.

Changes for the better are possible, but can come only from concerted effort by those who work at it, even though, especially at first, their numbers might be small. We *can* work together to heal the world, to make it a safer, happier place for ourselves, our children and those who follow. In fact, if we are to survive with a reasonable way of life we *must* work together with our neighbors around the world in the healing process. America cannot be healed without serious and sincere attention to healing the world.

Paul Simon said in his Introduction to <u>Healing America</u>:

> "The best way (for the United States) to be a beacon to the world is to keep on becoming our best selves....The positive values that we have inherited can be a quiet but powerful force for good. However, there is a big "if": if we combine those values with a vision of the kind of a nation and world we want, and then work for that vision....What kind of a world do you want to live in? What are you willing to do to achieve it?" He goes on to say, "Our national community of three hundred million is part of the world family of more than six billion. We lead militarily; we lead economically. Can we lead in values that will give our children a chance to live in a world of peace and justice and opportunity? Can we lead in sensitivity to those struggling to simply survive in much of the world?" (1)

Those are more than "sixty four dollar questions", and those questions are our challenge!

This book is divided into four Parts. Part I is a geographer's critical look at the world in the early years of the Twenty First Century. It develops the theme of "Our Troubled World of Extremes"

Part II identifies three key problems of our time, elaborated from Part I. Two of these problems are of immediate concern; the third, no less important, has longer term significance. If we can resolve these three, a big "if", other issues and problems will be easier to deal with.

Part III includes a brief history of "peace plans", the evolution of international cooperation over the last two centuries, the League of Nations and the United Nations. Part III lists hopeful signs supporting Limited World Government as well as arguments against, and presents three different approaches for establishing a Limited World Government. Part III also calls on people of all religions to help toward peace and justice for all and for a sustainable economic system.

Part IV, the Conclusion, draws attention to the urgency of solutions in our time and presents action suggestions for individuals. A "Web of Survival" is discussed and attention is called to the Athenians of ancient Greece.

If you are in a hurry to read what I have to say about world government you could skip to Parts III and IV, and return later to learn why the three critical issues I identify can be dealt with only on a global basis.

Although Paul Simon was the inspiration and immediate impetus for this book, he did not mention world government in his Healing America or his other books that I have read. Paul was a strong UN supporter and was keenly interested in cooperation among the nations. He also supported efforts of the Southern Illinois Chapter of the United Nations Association of the USA (UNA-USA), and especially encouraged us to reach out to develop interest among young people in our endeavor.

Healing the World is not meant to be a scholarly book. I have not included masses of numbers, graphs or and tables. For the most part I have used reasonably accessible materials in public libraries or on the Internet. The many quotes included demonstrate that critical problems about which I am writing have been acknowledged for a long time by many others. Based on my studies and thinking over many years, I have tried to convey what I believe is true about the issues discussed. Put very simply, the book's purpose is to help others learn about and put in perspective several critical and urgent issues of our time. I also hope many will see the importance of my writing and want to help with solutions.

Why am I proposing a World Government that is "Limited"? In this world of powerful nation-states the world government concept is likely to be considered only when the people convince their governments of the urgency of the problems I identify. Actions toward any world government movement would be considered only if that world government has limited powers. Powers and functions necessary for a viable world government are spelled out in Part III.

Even with Limited World Government, national governments would retain functions and powers they now have for managing domestic affairs within their borders. They would only give up some of their "sovereignty" in matters involving other nations, especially conflict resolution between the more powerful nations.

"Healing the World" has been written primarily for readers in the United States and especially for younger and older readers. Why focus on readers in the United States? Primarily because of the overwhelming economic and military power of our country. How Americans and our government respond to the theme of this book probably is more important than how others elsewhere react. The United States must lead the movement for world government! Citizens of other countries, mostly in Europe and with experience in organizing the European Union, seem to be more ready to consider seriously a world government approach to world peace. But without the United States joining in there could be problems.

And why especially for younger and older United States citizens? Our youth and young adults have been brought up during decades that focused too much on the individual in a hyped up world for consumers. For too many there never has been a concern for communities and the world. Because of the many obvious complex issues that swirl around them the idealism of many has been blunted. Younger "Americans" need a new goal away from "Me Firstism" and back to cooperation with others, a new goal to give their lives meaning and improve their future. And a rekindling of their concern for others must translate into political action. That action could be in support of Limited World Government.

Many older Americans who have retired from a lifetime of hard work focus attention on their children and grandchildren. And that is as it should be! They also may spend hours reading, watching TV, playing golf or bridge, traveling, other pleasant activities—and going to doctors!—while their retirement years slip by. Perhaps some of them need a "cause" to make their later years more meaningful. They could join the "cause" to bring on Limited World Government to help resolve the complex issues that face mankind. AARP could take it on as one of their priorities. The talents and support of those who are retired could make the lives of their children and those who follow more secure.

But will the United States cooperate in good faith with others? In our attempts to "protect" ourselves against terrorists, do we keep planting seeds for more terrorist attacks? Will we continue our bellicose and arrogant ways? So much of what will happen in the next decades is up to how United States citizens vote and how we relate to the rest of the world.

All of us are carriers of what we might call "cultural baggage". Every citizen of the world has grown up in a country and a culture and takes that culture for granted. Each of us grows up accepting that the way things are done in our home, church, school, community and nation are the "right" ways. After all, our "culture" has worked reasonably well for most of us and just about everyone around us seems to accept them.

But consider Aldous Huxley's point in the following quotation in which he reflects on his return from a journey, just as my wife, Carol, and I did on returns from our several overseas "journeys":

> "So the journey is over and I am back again where I started, richer by much experience and poorer by many exploded convictions, many perished certainties....I set out on my travels knowing, or thinking that I knew, how men should live, how be governed, how educated, what they should believe....Now, on my return, I find myself without any of these pleasing certainties....The better you understand the significance of any question, the more difficult it becomes to answer it....When one is traveling, convictions are mislaid as easily as spectacles; but unlike spectacles, they are not easily replaced." (2)

Most Americans have a skewed understanding of the rest of the world. Our media usually reports from overseas only news about wars and terrorists or unusual events. We learn very little about the every day problems and aspirations of ordinary people. In contrast, people in other countries know a great deal about the United States because much of what we do with our foreign policy and overseas business involves them in important ways.

In the spirit of Huxley's quote, I hope all readers of this volume will begin with an open mind. I hope readers will not pre-judge suggestions about how we might eliminate war from our lives, tame corporate globalization and develop a sustainable relationship with our Earth home. I hope my analysis of these urgencies that confront us, my explanation of three alternative approaches to setting up a world government, and my suggestions for elements needed for a successful world government will not be a hollow call, or a mere cry in the wilderness.

I hope readers will be convinced that adoption of world law through Limited World Government is the only intelligent way to approach the many global issues that face the human family. And I hope that for many readers the message of this book will be a call to action!

After World War II the idea of a world government *was* seriously considered around the globe. Numerous magazine articles and discussion groups explored world government as a way to achieve and maintain peace. Groups of scholars developed drafts of a World Constitution. The need for international law as the underpinning for resolving the war problem was widely discussed and well understood. In the midst of this interest in world government, in 1948 the people of Connecticut voted 12 to 1 to change the UN into a Limited World Government. (3) But a new enemy, the Cold War with the Soviet Union, pushed world government from the public's mind.

We need to revive the spirit and wisdom of those times and commit ourselves to the work of "healing the world". In 1980 Norman Cousins said,

> "The danger of nuclear war is the number-one problem. The number-two problem is that many of the best minds in our country are not focused on the number-one problem." (4).

If Norman Cousins could see our world today, I am quite confident he would agree that war and militarization are our number-one problem, and the number-two problem would still be that our leaders and most people are not focused on the number one problem! War and militarization and the "war on terrorism" rob us of our attention, time, money, lives and civil liberties. Furthermore, war, militarization and the "war on terrorism" can not provide real security. Being slaves to the war machine also prevents us from attending to other serious problems we face, including the real causes of terrorism.

As the world braced against the arms race between the United States and the Soviet Union from the 1950s to 1990, a very special booklet, edited by Harry Hollins, was published in 1958. The intriguing title of the booklet poses the question, "Can America Learn About Peace and Freedom From...." It includes forty three quotes from thirty world leaders, including five of our presidents, two Supreme Court justices, a Senator, Albert Einstein, Pope Pius XII, Winston Churchill, generals, historians, and Mayor Schinzo Hamai of Hiroshima.

Mayor Hamai's quote is the next to last in the booklet:

> "It is not my place to tell Americans what ought to be done. But what I can do is to tell them about what will happen to the world's cities if

something is not done to stop war....We know that stopping war is not a simple thing....We know, too, that peace is not to be had just for the asking: all nations must agree to it.

"But we also know that some nation must take leadership. America can call for world law, and all the world will listen....Let the call go out from America for a federation of the nations strong enough to prevent war, and a thrill will be known in the hearts of millions of people everywhere." (5)

And the last quote in the booklet is from Henry L. Stimson (Secretary of State under H. Hoover, Secretary of War under F. D. Roosevelt):

"How soon this nation will fully understand the size and nature of its present mission, I do not dare to say. But I venture to assert that in a very large degree the future of mankind depends on the answer to this question. And I am confident that if the issues are clearly presented, the American people will give the right answer." (6)

It is the purpose of this book to try to present those issues clearly so Americans will insist on the right answers that will lead to a more peaceful world for our children.

Ultimately, it is on behalf of our children and all those who will follow throughout the world that Paul wrote and for whom this retired geography professor and octogenarian is writing. I am satisfied that organizing a peaceful world with justice and opportunity is possible in the next decade or two. This won't be accomplished easily and there will be strong opposition. There will be sacrifices and set backs along the way. However, for all the impressive gains humans have achieved through the millennia to survive, we *must* eliminate war and solve other critical issues by adopting a Limited World Government—soon!

D.E.C., June 2005

PART I

OUR TROUBLED WORLD

Ours is a troubled world. Perhaps it has always been that way. There have been problems and challenges one way or another at least since human beings began to do things in ways different from other mammals. Until then, humans competed directly with other species for survival. The evolution of language, memory and brains gave early humans a critical edge, but still it was a hard and short life for most. Even with the impressive technological inventions and social advances that humans have achieved in recent centuries, unfortunately it is still a hard and rough life for most members of the human family today.

Only about one fourth of the human family enjoys a comfortable life, and in significant ways that comfortable life is based on the meager way of life of so many of our neighbors on this planet. I hope that many of those who are "doing well" have at least a small prick at their conscience on how their comfort depends on the work and resources of their neighbors in the less well off parts of the world. And I hope this book might help us work toward a world with less extremes.

Many of our troubles—and our wars—have derived from competing with others as our numbers have increased. We compete in using the Earth's limited resources and in making a living. We compete in our religions. We have very different concepts of ownership and in our responsibilities toward others and our Earth home. When our numbers were small such problems were limited and usually localized. Not so any more. When competition and conflict escalate the result has been regional or global war!

We all are passengers on a spaceship that is hurtling through space. Our spaceship has some critical problems, and our future and the future of our children and all future generations depend on whether and how we deal with those urgent problems. The title of Howard Zinn's autobiography, <u>You Can't Be Neutral on a Moving Train</u>, suggests our predicament on Earth: "…events are already moving in certain deadly directions, and to be neutral means you accept that." (1) No one should be neutral! As citizens of the world we all have a responsibility to help solve our problems while there is still time!

The purpose of Part One is to review how things are now. In effect it is a geographer's selective "primer of the world" in these early years of the twenty first century. It is a thumbnail sketch that touches on many problems but highlights three key problems the human family must face up to as we embark on this hope-laden century.

A. A WORLD OF EXTREMES

We live in a world of extremes, and it is becoming more polarized. In recent decades around the world the rich and the better off are getting richer and the poor are getting poorer. The rich are gaining more political power as middle classes struggle to get along and the poor are given little, if anything.

In the United States Congress there is little bipartisan effort on any issue, as each political party struggles to gain advantage over the other. The drive is "to win" in Congress and in elections at any cost. Although our country is split quite evenly between the two major parties, both parties have forgotten that a government's function is to help the general welfare of the people and that politics is the art of compromise. In recent years the uncompromising Congress of the United States has led to ill-advised actions as well as inaction on critical issues. And both have exacerbated problems in our troubled world!

More and more Americans seem to be "one issue" individuals when they go to the polls, with divisive religious issues being at the core of the concerns of many. This last point is surprising in a country that has as one of its founding principles the wise concept of "separation of church and state". This concept does not mean that individuals in our "secular" government should proceed with no ethical or moral underpinnings. Of course not! They must and do have ethical and moral underpinnings. We also should acknowledge that individuals who say they believe in God or have a religious affiliation does not guarantee moral or ethical behavior any more than having no religious affiliation indicates an immoral or amoral person.

Another way to demonstrate our world of extremes is to divide countries into two generalized groups: the "Haves" and the "Have-nots". The "Haves" represent about one-fourth of the world's population; the "Have-nots" about three-fourths. The "Haves" are the better-off world, fulfilling their needs at least partly off the cheap labor and resources of the poorer world. And the "Have-nots" are the not-very-well-off world, those countries and areas struggling to "develop" and make improvements for their people. Of course this is an over-simplification because some countries and areas are "in between".

Thumbnail descriptions of these two very different but interdependent worlds are listed in <u>Appendix A</u>. The two lists are titled "Three-fourths of the World" and "One-Fourth of the World" and roughly represent three-fourths and one-fourth of the world's people. Listed for each of these two "worlds" are fourteen points that describe environmental, educational, religious, urban, government and other characteristics in a general way. For easy comparison related points on both the "Three-fourths of the World" and "One-Fourth of the World" lists are numbered the same in adjoining columns.

These two worlds are intertwined and depend on each other. In most of the richer countries there are pockets of poverty in many cities and in rural areas that have been left behind by social and technological advances. In the poorer countries there are elites of the educated, wealthy and powerful who live well in European-like cities and neighborhoods amidst their struggling neighbors, many who live in shanty-towns.

These lists help us understand the bipolar nature of our "world of extremes". It is clear from the lists that things are not going well for most among three-fourths of the human family. We also can see there are urgent problems for those in the better-off countries or elites as well.

In decades past "Have-not" countries and areas have been called: "undeveloped", "underdeveloped", "backward", "primitive", "uncivilized", and all of these terms carry negative connotations. To avoid any negative connotation, for decades I have used the term "Technologically Less-Advanced areas" (or "TLA") for the less developed countries and areas and "Technologically Advanced areas" (or "TA") for the "West", or countries and areas that are more technologically advanced. These terms and their abbreviations "TA" and "TLA" are used several times throughout this book.

Lester Pearson, who became Prime Minister of Canada, in 1957 made the following very important observation about a key change that took place after World War II in the aspirations of TLA countries and areas:

> "It is already difficult to realize that a mere twenty years ago poverty was taken almost for granted over most of the earth's surface. There were always, of course, a few visionaries, but before 1939, there was little practical consideration given to the possibility of raising the living standards of Asia and Africa in the way that we now regard as

indispensable. Perhaps only in North America every man feels entitled to a motor car, but in Asia hundreds of millions of people do
now expect to eat and be free. They no longer will accept colonialism, destitution and distress as preordained. That may be the most
significant of all revolutionary changes in the international social
fabric of our times."(2)

Barbara Ward echoed the same concern in a more sinister fashion in 1972:

"Either (nations) will move on to a community based upon more
systematic sharing of wealth—through progressive income tax,
through general policies of education, shelter, health, and housing—
or they will break down in revolt and anarchy." (3)

And a Presidential Commission on World Hunger had this to say in its 1979
report to the President:

"The most explosive force in the world today is the frustrated desire
of poor people to attain a decent standard of living. The anger,
despair, and often hatred that result represent a real and persistent
threat to international order. No monetary value can be placed on
avoiding the chaos that will ensue unless the United States and the
rest of the world begin to develop a common institutional framework for meeting such critical global threats as the growing scarcity
of fossil fuels and other non-renewable resources, environmental
pollution and international terrorism. This combination of problems threatens the national security of all countries just as surely as
advancing armies or nuclear arsenals." (4)

These three quotes represent the most profound change that has taken place in
the dynamics of international relations in the last half century. Even now leaders of most nations do not understand or fully appreciate their implications
that change virtually everything!

These three quotes, therefore, are among the most important in this book. I
include them—in chronological order—to emphasize that for decades a
potential problem—even terrorism—has been acknowledged if the advances
and comforts of those living in TA countries are not shared with those less fortunate. The basis of that threat was—and is—known as "the Revolution of
Rising Expectations" among the world's less well-off people. Prior to World
War II little thought was given to the difficult life situations of most on this
planet. With further technological advances, especially in communications,

that is not the case now. These three quotes touch on the real seeds for the terrorism that is manifest around the world in recent decades!

We also should ponder the truth in a brief quote (from the Internet) by Sir Peter Ustinov: "Terrorism is the war of the poor, and war is the terrorism of the rich."

The "Revolution of Rising Expectations" includes both positive and negative aspects. On the one hand it is encouraging that the colonial world of the last two centuries was dismantled after World War II. It also is encouraging that so many people in TLA countries, especially since World War II, are struggling for more education for their children, for health care, and a better way of life for themselves and their families. However, on the other hand, even with the dismantling of Europe's colonial empires since World War II, countries of the TA "West" have not reduced their economic domination of TLA areas; in fact they have increased it.

Furthermore, there are harsh realities about our Earth that put a ceiling on "rising expectations". Rich and varied as are the Earth's resources, many very obviously are limited and are not equally distributed around the Earth. Even more critical to the future of our planet and the human family, there are not enough resources to provide to all of the world's people—even now—with necessities and a level of living equal to the average in "the West". That is why population control measures are so critical for all passengers on Spaceship Earth!

With our hyper advertising and movies we are teaching the rest of the world about our super consumerism and our generally comfortable way of life, and we are implicitly inviting them to join in our affluence. But there is little chance they can gain that prize in their own countries. That is why so many, especially the more able and daring, would like to move to Europe, the United States or Canada. But for those who cannot come to "the West" life can turn bitter, as we know from 9/11/2001 as well as prior and subsequent acts of terror.

Another key point needs to be emphasized from the two lists in Appendix A. Each physical, social and economic aspect of every part of the world must be understood in relation to all other items on those lists. Each item is part of a cause of or effect on other items. It is virtually impossible to deal effectively with one element of the social situation or economy in any TLA or TA country without involving many other items.

For instance, one cannot deal realistically with malnutrition or a health issue in a TLA country without becoming entangled with subsistence agriculture, low incomes, health care, transportation and communication facilities, rapid population growth, limited tax base, limited education, national indebtedness, as well as resource endowments that also pose serious limitations. In similar fashion, a web of interrelations among characteristics of TA nations also would instruct us about the complexity of solving problems in TA countries and areas. We must keep these "webs of interrelationships" in mind as we contemplate solutions to the many and varied problems that plague us.

For thousands of years Earth's bourgeoning human family has taken more and more resources of all kinds from our Earth home. Farms lands have been pressed harder and harder. Grand civilizations and empires have come and gone, partly through unwitting misuse of their resources. In our time, through fertilizers, pesticides, hybrids and hormones, production of food and fiber has increased dramatically in many parts of the world.

The "Green Revolution" of the 1970s, brought on by use of fertilizers and genetically altered rice and wheat seeds, comes to mind as a well-intentioned program that helped some farmers. However, most TLA farmers could not benefit from the Green Revolution for lack of money. Substantially increasing crop yields by genetics or other means cannot go on indefinitely. Even now water run-off from farms carrying fertilizer, pesticide residue and animal waste is seriously polluting surface and ground water resources in the United States and elsewhere.

We hear much these days about the need for a "sustainable" economic system, which means, simply, that for the long term stability of the future of the human family, we must organize our use of the Earth's resources in ways that will sustain all forms of life indefinitely. That last point is critical. "Sustainable" should mean forever and for all forms of life, not just humans and those forms of life we choose not to exterminate. Anything less and we are not being fair to our children and those who will follow. The basic challenge of population control is on the table: the world has insufficient resources and productive capacity to support over six billion humans at "the West's" level of living.

It is clear that we live in a world that is bipolar in terms of the sharp division between TA and TLA countries. However, the tragedy for our time is that the differences between them are NOT decreasing. The poorer areas are increasing in population and becoming more poverty stricken, with all of the potential for violent release of unfulfilled expectations and hopes. People in the wealthier countries are gaining in wealth and power and are becoming more concerned about immigration issues.

Witness construction of the "Tortilla Wall" (the "Berlin-like" and "Israeli-like" wall) being built along our southern California border to try to keep Mexicans from illegally entering the United States. The increasing gaps between rich and poor do not bode well for a stable future for the world. Even after decades of foreign aid being given by TA countries, an improved way of life is not being generated in most TLA areas.

An article by Bruce Scott in the Jan.-Feb. 2001 <u>Foreign Affairs</u> touches on several of the points included in the TLA characterization. He said the economic globalization of recent decades

> "offers opportunities for all nations, but most developing (TLA) countries are very poorly positioned to capitalize on them. Malarial climates, limited access to navigable water, long distances to major markets, and unchecked population growth are only part of the problem. Such countries also have very unequal income structures inherited from colonial regimes, and these patterns of income distribution are hard to change unless prompted by a major upheaval such as a war or a revolution. But as serious as these disadvantages are, the greatest disadvantage has been the poor quality of government." (5)

Another very telling perspective on our "World of Extremes" was the subject of an anonymous item, "Summary of the World", in an Ann Landers column in 1997:

> "If we could shrink the Earth's population to a village of precisely 100 people, with all existing human ratios remaining the same, it would look like this:
> There would be 57 Asians, 21 Europeans, 14 from North and South America, and eight from Africa.
> Fifty-one would be female, 49 would be male.
> Seventy would be non-white, while 30 would be white.
> Sixty-six would be non-Christian and 33 Christian.
> Eighty would live in substandard housing.
> Seventy would be unable to read.
> Half would suffer from malnutrition.
> One would be near death, and one would be near birth.
> Only one would have a college education.

> Half of the entire village's wealth would be in the hands of only six people, and all six would be citizens of the United States." (6)

Although this was written in 1997, a 2004 summary would look about the same and carry the same message of "extremes" and the "Revolution of Rising Expectations".

B. HISTORICAL PERSPECTIVE

Long before humans evolved, their pre-human forebears got along with the strongest being the leaders. As larger groups became organized a "critical mass" may have been achieved which stimulated human thinking, memory and genius. Thinking, reasoning, cleverness, memory and then language became more valued over brute strength in survival and getting things done.

We congratulate ourselves as creatures with brains and reasoning power. However, the record is not good even now on whether individuals make important decisions in their lives from the reality of facts, for selfish and self-serving reasons, by their emotions, or by delusional notions that are implanted by the media—even during election campaigns! We must use our reason and our compassion if we are to make changes that must be made to solve in time the world wide problems that are before us.

There *are* solutions to the critical problems we face. Development of these solutions obviously must start with the present condition of the Earth and resources the Earth offers now. Solutions also must involve the whole human family if there is to be any reasonable future for our children and those who follow. With high levels of interdependence, there can be no successful effort by any single nation to solve problems only within its borders. And there can be no successful solutions to the world's problems under the domination of one country.

We are at a critical time in the history of homo sapiens on Earth. We must learn fast how to work with others as we never have before! Most cultures and nations have carried over attitudes and ideas from the past, ideas that have blocked working with others to solve problems. These cultural blocks must be abandoned so we can deal with the critical issues of today. Whether the world's people and governments can do this in the next decade or two as caring beings will dictate whether the human experiment on this planet will move on to greatness or face the threat of world wide revolution and environmental crisis leading to another Dark Age.

Certain problems are so critical to our future and are so intertwined with others on the Earth that most of them must be faced and resolved together. Accepting that as our situation, how do we start to deal with these problems and where is there money enough to begin facing up to them?

Every country has powerful special interests that are advantaged by the status quo. We should acknowledge that solutions will shake up and challenge some of the most powerful and long-standing special interests everywhere. The fact that applying solutions will shake up special interests no doubt explains our not having applied those solutions before! There can be no "sacred cows"! Solutions to the most critical problems will open doors and make possible resolving our other important challenges.

One such special interest involves the entrenched power of the world's military establishment and all of the corporations, businesses, communities and individuals who feed it and are supported by it in one way or another. The United States has more military power and military business than most other nations combined and therefore its economy and way of life would feel the greatest repercussions if we make moves to reduce it in its many manifestations.

"The military?" you say, "How can we get along without it?" The military by its very nature cannot solve problems. Put very simply, the mission of the military is to kill and destroy "an enemy". Wars and conflicts only change temporarily the relations between and among the leading players on the world's chessboard. On behalf of one nation or several, the military uses violence and destruction and deception in response to real or hyped up problems. At the end of every conflict the participants must always gather around a table and work out some kind of resolution of the problems or situation that brought on the conflict. "Victor" and vanquished also must deal with the deaths, desolation, destruction and bankruptcy that wars bring. I put "victor" in parentheses because in reality in modern war there are no victors. But is there any other way to resolve problems between nations?

We can learn from history: Homo sapiens started on Earth in small struggling family units, clans and tribes. By consolidation these small units were able to increase their security. By further consolidations into still larger units and to the nation states we know today, greater security was made possible within larger and larger areas as rules of conduct and laws evolved. The larger units with internal security also multiplied the ability of humans to innovate, invent and express themselves through the arts. And concepts like democracy and human rights were born.

At present we have consolidated to the level of nations, and we have seen a flowering of human ingenuity in so many ways. However, we are still stuck to the past on the important issue of security between nations. Despite talk about "international law" between nations there still is anarchy. We have moved into an age of utter interdependence among all people on this planet. We depend on each other in so many ways. No country is self-sufficient. No community is self-sufficient. We all depend on many things we obtain from other parts of the globe to maintain a particular way of life. And yet we have not followed our own experience. We have not implemented the only sure way to provide security between the nation-units that cover the Earth. That way is to enlarge the area that functions under law.

C. LIMITED WORLD GOVERNMENT

The next step is to a Limited World Government. We should look on this crucial next step as an opportunity to adopt a global strategy that will help solve the most pressing problems facing humanity. These three problems are: the problem of war itself, corporate globalization, and the need for a sustainable balance between our Earth home and its human family.

Our forebears in thirteen colonies faced a similar challenge over two centuries ago. Leaders in those days saw the practicality of their joining together to resist their colonial masters and solve other problems. For the first few years these thirteen independent colonies dabbled with a confederate form of central government, which did not solve their problems. In 1787 they developed the Constitution that set up a central government—with limited powers—above the thirteen colonial governments. That Constitution with its amendments still serves all Americans today!

Over most of last century people and nations of the world, in an effort to abolish war, have dabbled with the League of Nations and the United Nations. Both were established as confederacies, voluntary organizations of nations with no real powers over their members. Member nations who join confederacies retain all of their "so-called sovereign powers" and can withdraw or say "no" at any time.

I say "so-called sovereign powers" because, with the level of interdependence so high among nations, no nation is really "sovereign" any more. Sovereignty is ballyhooed by politicians all the time but in today's world it is a myth from a bygone age. We are one nation among many nations that depend on each other in so many ways.

We should be very aware that even the United States with all of its riches in natural resources and its economic and military power does not and cannot (and should not) have its way among nations. Our "way of life" depends on trade with many countries around the world, both TA and TLA. Without trade our diet would be much less varied during much of each year. Without trade for critical metals there would be far fewer computers, automobiles, trucks, and airplanes. Our cities would be more compact. Air travel would be very limited. There would be far fewer autos as more of us would depend on walking, bicycles and public transportation!

The more fortunate humans living in "the West" have dominated the world for several centuries and, with our more mature governments, our greater prosperity and attention to the "finer things in life", we call ourselves "civilized". However the United States by itself has enough military power to destroy anything mankind has made on Earth. We also have atomic and other bombs that could destroy all mammals and birds on Earth. Humans have adopted ways that over time could render the Earth unfit to support humans and many forms of life.

Globalization is coming whether we see it, like it or understand it. World population is burgeoning and global warming is happening whether some government "leaders" acknowledge it or not. World reserves of fossil fuels are dwindling and development of new alternatives must be given top priority. Wasteful and debilitating wars to control petroleum reserves during their last dwindling decades are the acts of fools.

Considering all of this, should we call ours a "civilization"? Is a real world wide "civilization" even possible, given the great differences among the world's people and nations and the problems we face? Can we rational humans do better than we are doing now and reduce the extremes we see around the Earth?

My answer to those last two questions is "yes". We can do better, and the key is to back away from our dependence on the military and deal realistically with several critical problems that are here now. Nations and people working together to establish Limited World Government is the key. Money saved from military expenditures is a "Peace Dividend" that can help deal with other problems. These changes could lead to the world's first true "global civilization".

We are at the threshold of a desperately needed new age, "The Age of Globalization". If we do not measure up to this challenge, if we go about our business as usual, a continuation of present policies will temporarily, and I repeat, only temporarily enrich the privileged few while the problems of the many and our Earth home are ignored. Terrorism will increase, democracies will be further compromised, and a new Dark Age is likely.

Given all that has happened over the last century to bring us to our present situation, the challenge for today's adult generations is to help this new age come on in ways that will assure a reasonable and sustainable future for our children and those who will follow.

PART II

THREE KEY PROBLEMS

Part I of this volume presented a generalized summary of our "bipolar world of extremes" with some attention to issues that need solution if we are seeking a better world for all. Since the beginning of the human experiment on Earth, each generation has inherited a problem-ridden world from the generation that came before. However, unless we take action now, we will hand down to our children even more difficult problems than were handed to us.

We must not pass on to them a poisoned world with wars and stresses and monumental debts to repay, a world with critical social and economic problems and deep-seated ethnic and other issues. We must not pass on to them an Earth so damaged by human actions that our children's lives will be ridden with problems. If we leave all of these problems for them to face we will have failed them as caring parents and grandparents.

But can we start to fix the world so our children will be less burdened with problems from our generation? Can we at least begin to heal the Earth's many wounds? Wars will continue until human beings come to their senses and develop the social machinery and institutions that will set war aside forever. The rich and powerful will continue to take advantage of those who are weaker unless we the people act to make changes. It will be far easier for us to develop the necessary institutions to deal with these issues now and not leave it for problems to get worse and for our children to solve.

If we do nothing about war, globalization, environmental and other issues—in a few short years and by the time the world belongs to our children—we will have wasted trillions more dollars on militarization and more wars, and thousands more innocents will have needlessly been sacrificed. The phenomenon of globalization, that now primarily benefits multinational corporations, will have become so entrenched around the world that it will be much more difficult to rein in and control. And solutions to all problems, including establishing a sustainable balance between the bourgeoning human family and our Earth home, will be more complicated and expensive to apply.

But solving problems is not easy. To solve a problem one first must acknowledge there IS a problem. Then solutions require careful thinking and acknowledgement of consequences if no action is taken. Reconciliation, discussion, and perhaps some compromise are the actions nations must take to overcome differences and solve problems.

Three key problems have been selected from those mentioned in Part I: 1. GOVERNMENT AND WAR, 2. CORPORATE GLOBALIZATION, and 3. THE EARTH AND PEOPLE. These have been selected because in the judgment of this writer they are the most critical and pervasive issues facing the human family in our time. The first two are immediate challenges. The third also is as critical as the first two for the longer-term viability and security of the human experiment on Earth.

If we can focus on these, and hopefully put them on the road toward solution, other issues noted in Part I will become solvable.

A. GOVERNMENT AND WAR

"The whole of recorded history is a history of the expansion of states as the means of communication increased, so that there has been a continual extension of law systems. In the past third of a century, this expansion has reached its climax, so that the double aspect of life, home and foreign, has at last disappeared. All war is now civil war. The sluggish general intelligence has still to grasp the fact. World unity under a common law is now the only alternative to chaos." (1)

H. G. Wells wrote those words in 1941 when Britain expected Germany to invade. You must reread the last sentence. These words are as relevant today as they were then. They summarize humanity's struggle for peace through international law.

As Howard Zinn put it more recently:

"...war brutalizes everyone involved, begets a fanaticism in which the original moral factor....is buried at the bottom of a heap of atrocities committed by all sides....By the 1960s, my old belief in a 'just war' was falling apart. I was concluding that while there are certainly vicious enemies of liberty and human rights in the world, war itself is the most vicious of enemies. (2)

Note that he said "atrocities committed by all sides" and be reminded of Guantanamo and Abu Ghraib.

Many generals, presidents and world leaders have spoken about the wastefulness of war, the tragedy of war, the uncontrollability of war, and the foolishness of war that goes against everything civilization stands for. Here and later in the book are several from various Internet sources, including <www.voteworldgovernment.org/quotes.shtml>.

General and President Ulysses S. Grant on March 4, 1873: "I believe that our Great Maker is preparing the world, in His own good time, to become one nation, speaking one language, when armies and navies will no longer be required."

General Douglas MacArthur: "You cannot control war, you can only abolish it. Those who shrug this off as idealistic are the real enemies of peace, the real war mongers."

General and President Dwight Eisenhower: "War in our time has become an anachronism. Whatever the case in the past, war in the future can serve no useful purpose."

Prime Minister Winston Churchill in May 1947: "If, during the next five years, it is found possible to build a world organization of irresistible force and inviolable authority for the purpose of securing peace, there are no limits to the blessings which all men may enjoy and share."

Reverend Martin Luther King: "We must learn to live together as brothers or perish together as fools."

1. LIES AND MISINFORMATION. The United States became deeply involved in Vietnam in 1964 because of the "Gulf of Tonkin" resolution that was passed by the Congress. Years later it was acknowledged that the "Gulf of Tonkin incident" was a lie. The American destroyers that were supposedly attacked by North Korean torpedo boats were not attacked at all, much less in international waters, as our military and President Johnson had insisted. Nevertheless, the Gulf of Tonkin lie was used to commit the U.S. to a long and costly war in Vietnam with massive casualties on both sides, until the U.S. finally pulled out in 1975.

During President Reagan's administration in the 1980s military equipment, armament and even banned chemicals were sold to Saddam Hussein to help in his fight with Iran. We know, too, that Donald Rumsfeld was an important negotiator in these transactions. We know also that Reagan used funds from illegal arms sales to Iran to support mercenaries in Nicaragua (the "contra") to oust Daniel Ortega, Nicaragua's popular, fairly elected president who, despite accusations, was not a "Communist". But more on that later.

For months in 2002 President George W. Bush and his inner circle insisted that Saddam Hussein had "weapons of mass destruction" he was likely to use on the United States soon. We know now that was a lie, even though it was used to justify the United States' preemptive invasion of Iraq. We know also there was no evidence to support Bush's further charge that Saddam had been a supporter of the al-Qaida terrorist organization. We also now know that "intelligence reports" were adjusted to fit the president's plan to invade Iraq.

The United States take-over of Hawaii in 1893, "Remember the Alamo" in 1835, "Remember the Maine" in 1893, sending our marines into Central and Latin American countries over and over in the late 1800s and early 1900s to "protect American interests", the Pueblo incident with North Korea in 1968, the Granada invasion in 1983, the Panama invasion in 1989 and other incidents raise serious questions about how our country has become involved in conflicts and gone to war on the basis of questionable information, or simply for "business" or diversion reasons. And some of these incidents and invasions brought deadly results to many innocents, including some of our own.

Lies, misinformation and decisions to protect American businesses overseas have been made by Republican and Democratic presidents, so it is a problem that goes deeper than party politics. It goes to the heart of a democracy that depends on its citizens (and its Congress!) to be truthfully informed and to participate in making good decisions when they vote. James Warburg goes further on this point regarding post-World War II years. Consider how the Iraq war was presented to the American people and Congress as you read his quote about our four decades arms race with the Soviet Union:

> "…national policy has not been explained to the Congress and the people. It has been 'sold' by an appeal to fear and hatred rather than by an appeal to reason….The policy of secrecy, of non-disclosure, and the dishing out of unwarranted reassurances, instead of factual information, destroys the very foundation of democracy, which is an alert and informed citizenry. (3)

Many millions elsewhere in the world know well our lies and deceit. Furthermore, with knowledge of the lies and misinformation that involved our country in conflicts over the years, and after the clouds of doubt raised by recent elections in the United States, it is understandable that millions of Americans also are cynical and "turned off" about our democracy and election processes. Younger people especially seem to be turned off from voting and becoming involved to help their communities. Perhaps they can be reinvigorated by joining efforts toward "healing the world" and establishing a Limited World Government.

On the Internet I found quotes from two recent presidents who had encouraging things to say about our country's future and the UN. After the disintegration of the Soviet Union and before the first Gulf War (when we still had hope for a "peace dividend"!), George Herbert Walker Bush, the father of President George W. Bush, said:

> "We have before us the opportunity to forge for ourselves and for future generations a new world order—a world where the rule of law, not the law of the jungle, governs the conduct of nations....an order in which a credible United Nations can use its peacekeeping role to fulfill the promise and vision of the United Nation's founders." (Jan. 16, 1991.) (4)

And President Clinton said,

> "I want to assure all of you....that, as President I will work closely with the international community through the United Nations and other vital institutions to resolve the contentious disputes and to meet the challenges of the next century." (Jan. 18, 1993) (7)

It is sad that both of these statements of good intention were contradicted by what those presidents actually did while in office. No doubt their hopes were set aside as they encountered the powerful influence of the military in our government and way of life. President Jimmy Carter campaigned that he would reduce the military budget, but in office he increased it, no doubt for the same reason.

2. VIOLENCE LEADS TO MORE VIOLENCE. The military path has never brought long-term security and peace to the world or any part of it. Whatever the problem or geopolitical dispute, violence leads to more violence. Wars waste everything we value, even to setting aside basic ideals and democratic principles in order to confront an "enemy". Regardless of who "wins" or "loses", in modern warfare just about everyone is a loser in lives lost, injuries, destruction, money and resources.

However, war and militarization do provide employment for many, including many communities. Wars enrich war-related businesses, and pressure from lobbyists and military contractors may be why wars and militarization persist. War also seems to feed the male ego and encourage male bonding. But wars are bitter for the losers; they solve no problems, and the bitterness can fester for generations. Making an "enemy" out of a competitor or opponent blocks all reasonable communication toward solving a problem. Those labeled "terrorists" or "insurgents" by some are revered as "freedom fighters" and "martyrs" by others. Consider how American colonial "patriots" would have been portrayed in England during our Revolution.

At the end of any war (or revolution) the problems that brought it on are still there, along with new problems and the devastation. While facing all of their losses, victor and vanquished still must try to reach some kind of workable solution and move on. We should have learned by now that violent means can not lead to a peaceful world.

The vast majority of Americans are kind and caring people. We want to trust our neighbors, not fear them. We want to help those in need. We want our government to be straightforward with us, not deceive us. As a people we are simultaneously progressive in our social impulses and fiscally conservative in wanting our tax money to be spent wisely. We are willing to accept changes that will help our country and the world to be better places for all.

My commenting on controversial issues from our past and the potential of Limited World Government are grounded in my firm belief in the basic ideals of our country and the promise of America to its people and the people of the world.

Even without actual wars, during so-called "peacetime", expensive militarization goes on apace in most countries as security is vainly sought. When confrontation finally leads to war, more civilians are killed than military personnel. Military action also destroys everything people need to survive. It is pathetic that war and militarization do all this without being able to provide anyone with real security, and is even more pathetic that so few seem to "connect the dots" and understand this!

The business of war is to kill and destroy "the enemy". How pathetic it is that when a war comes most church leaders go along with government edicts and propaganda. They pray for the troops, they pray for victory, and pray to God to be on their side (in eliminating the enemy). One wonders how Christians reconcile this with the Fifth Commandment and with Jesus' message of love and compassion for others.

"War and Militarization" is so pervasive in the United States that "feeding the military" for past, present and future wars dominate our national budget and priorities. There are military bases and military contracts in small and large businesses in every state and many counties, and for many counties and cities these are their basis for survival. In dozens of countries around the world the United States has thousands of military personnel. These military operations also employ large numbers of United States citizens and many from the individual countries.

With so many jobs on the line, it will be difficult to wean the United States from its military addiction. But it must be done if we want to maintain (or recover?) a healthy democracy. Witness the lobbying pressure that accompanies discussion about closure of any military base in our country! It would be a sad and immoral acknowledgement that we maintain our military establishment in part simply as a "jobs program".

For decades our government and military industries have been among the largest distributors and sales agents of military equipment and training around the world. Our government sells or gives away older military equipment to cement relationships with particular "friendly" nations. Perhaps it also is done to intimidate potential "enemies". A large part of our "foreign aid" is in the form of military equipment and training. Spreading more war machines and training around the world obviously does not lead to world peace and stability.

Furthermore, our experience with Iraq shows how tenuous that "friendly" designation might be. It was mentioned that during the 1980 Reagan years Donald Rumsfeld helped negotiate with Saddam Hussein for the United States to provide military materials to help Iraq fight Iran! The Reagan administration also looked the other way when Saddam Hussein used gas on his own Kurdish citizens. And in February 2003 Rumsfeld led our military in the United States' preemptive ousting of Saddam Hussein! Our president then undertook looking for "Weapons of Mass Destruction" (WMDs), some of which our government knew Saddam did have because we had delivered them to him in the 1980s.

3. PEOPLE WANT TO LIVE IN PEACE. The vast majority of humans want to live peaceably with others and we have invented government and laws to make this possible. For our "civilized" way of life we want and need many services, like police and fire protection, public schools, parks, pure water and sewer services, and many more. These cost money and we pay taxes to provide those services it would be difficult to provide for ourselves.

In his Parable of the Tribes Andrew Schmookler helps us understand how humans, perhaps since our tribal beginnings, have had their desire to live peaceably with others forcibly set aside by aggressive neighbors.

> "The tyranny of power is such that even self-defense becomes a kind of surrender. Not to resist is to be transformed at the hands of the mighty. To resist requires that one transform oneself into their *(aggressive and brutal)* likeness. Either way, free human choice is

prevented. All ways but the ways of power are blocked."(6) (Word in *italics* is mine. D.E.C.)

Schmookler goes on to say:

> "The essence of freedom is the ability to choose that which one wants. When people can act on the basis of such freedom, what they do and what they make are true expressions of themselves…The parable of the tribes argues that throughout evolution of civilization, human beings have been robbed of that freedom. And it maintains, consequently, that civilization as we see it in history is neither the fruit of human choice nor a reflection of human nature." (7)

Although the Bible and Koran give mixed messages on the matter of killing "non-believers", religions generally teach us it is wrong to kill other people and to be compassionate to those in need. Yet the record of our governments in helping those in need is not a positive one. Actions of the G. W. Bush administration are squeezing the middle class down and increasing the number of poor in the United States. And most foreign aid is designed to help businesses at home (including armament makers) even more than it helps those in poverty overseas. It also is easy to understand how violent computer games and movies can neutralize peaceful tendencies and encourage, especially among the young, acceptance of violence and killing as "normal".

In contradiction to our learning at an early age in home and church that it is wrong to kill, people later are taught that it is not only all right but necessary to kill "enemies" during war. It is easy enough for governments by patriotic hype and lies to brainwash people to fear, hate and kill some of their neighbors on this planet who have been designated as "enemies", usually those who have a different skin color or beliefs.

In a May 1991 column titled, "Choosing Wisely in Matters of War: Some lessons from History", Paul Simon expressed his concerns about the first President Bush's Gulf War and quoted Herman Goering, Hitler's number two man. Goering had this to say at his Nuremberg trial following World War II:

> "Why, of course, people don't want war. Why should some poor slob on a farm want to risk his life in a war when the best he can get out of it is to come back to his farm in one piece?…Naturally, the common people don't want war; neither in Russia, nor in England, nor for that matter in Germany. That is understood. But after all, it is the leaders of the country who determine the policy, and it is always a

simple matter to drag the people along, whether it is a democracy, or a parliament, or a communist dictatorship. Voice or no voice, the people can always be brought to the bidding of the leaders. That is easy. All you have to do is tell them they are being attacked, and denounce the pacifist for lack of patriotism and exposing the country to danger. It works the same in any country." (8)

Are people such pawns or sheep? Our leaders surely do have control of the message as to who is an enemy and who are friends, but even those change with time. Witness changes in status of Japan, German, Iran and Iraq over the decades! Heinrich Goering's quote is well worth pondering.

There are times when prompt military intervention is needed to stop a genocidal pogrom somewhere in the world. However, that *should* be one of the responsibilities of the UN or a "Global Peace Force", which is discussed later. Hindsight always is a more accurate vantage point from which to assess the right and courageous response that should have been made. For example, had President Roosevelt granted asylum to the boatload of Jews who were released from Nazi Germany early in World War II, it might have sent a signal that would have changed German policy. And had President Clinton given United States backing for an early UN response to the 1994 Hutu genocide in Rwanda, that tragedy might have been stopped before 200,000 or more Tutsis had been killed. Clinton's inaction flies in the face of his 1993 inaugural commitment (quoted earlier) to work closely with the UN to resolve disputes. As I write, the UN has been unable to garner support to respond to the genocidal killings and village destruction that began in Sudan's Darfur province in 2003 by the "Janjaweed" terrorists who have the support of Sudan's government.

The world-wide pattern seems to be that governments (including our own) look the other way when a dispute is a "people issue" only. But if a dispute involves corporate interests or key resources an outside government wants, then action comes down hard on whoever is in the way.

Some folks look back to the 1950—1990 "cold war" as a time of successful foreign policy and without bloodshed by the arms race between the United States and the Soviet Union. During those decades the UN was used by both the United States and the Soviet Union to further their world agendas. "Anti-Communism" was the focal point of United States foreign and domestic policy from World War II to the break-up of the Soviet Union in 1990.

In his years as president, Ronald Reagan pushed the arms race with the Soviet Union and tripled our national debt. For four decades the arms race kept the two most powerful nations at bay in an intense and costly stand off, which in the end did bankrupt the Soviet Union. However, these decades cannot be counted as the military providing "peace and security". The Cold War decades were years of a "balance of terror". They were years of construction of bomb shelters in both countries, of people hoarding caches of food and water in a closet or "under the stairs" in case of an attack, and of school children undergoing routine practices crawling under their desks in case of a bombing. Everyone lived under the sword of Damocles.

Although the arms race did not drive the United States into bankruptcy, that enormous debt is a legacy with which our children and grandchildren will have to deal. President Clinton started us on the road to control our national deficit and national debt (one year to year, the other long-term), but President George W. Bush's tax cuts, largely for the wealthy plus mounting expenses for his pre-emptive off-budget Iraq war, are leaving us still deeper in debt with consequences that are edging us toward bankruptcy and problems for our grandchildren and beyond!

In March 1991 at the close of the brief Iraq-Kuwait war, Paul Simon wrote about the challenges facing the United States and the world because of that war. How right he was then AND now!

"We know already that the hostility toward the United States in the Muslim world has grown since the shooting began on January 16th (1991). A major challenge for American diplomacy now that the war is over, will be to demonstrate our willingness to help those we have fought, and those outside Iraq who cheered Saddam. It will not be an easy undertaking, but we must make the effort for the sake of lasting stability in that volatile part of the world.

"It is already clear that the Arab and Western coalition partners will have an opportunity to move on some of the region's outstanding problems. Those problems extend beyond the obvious ones of peace between Iraq and Kuwait, and between Israel and her Arab neighbors.

"Other major concerns include the virtual absence of democracy in the Middle East, with the notable exception of Israel; the proliferation of nuclear, chemical and biological weapons; access to fresh water supplies and the possible conflicts that could arise from water scarcity; the many religious and sectarian disputes that have long plagued the Middle East; numerous border conflicts; and the huge economic disparities between countries and peoples within countries. As the leader in the war against Iraq, the United States should also lead in resolving these long-festering problems. And we ought to help build the peace as we have fought the war, hand-in-glove with the United Nations, one of he positive legacies of this whole affair." (9)

The "anti-terrorism" policies of President George W. Bush dominated and affected all programs and politics during his first term as president. Our country in effect became "Fortress America". The Patriot Act was bulldozed through Congress in haste in 2001, a few weeks after the 9/11 attacks. It is acknowledged that few members of Congress had a chance to read it or even reflect on its hundreds of pages.

Like the Alien and Sedition Acts of the early 1800s, Bush's post 9/11 "Patriot Act" curtailed civil liberties. "Homeland Security" costs placed heavy extra burdens on states and communities already struggling with reduced budgets. At first security measures discouraged many individuals from traveling, especially abroad. And our President tried repeatedly and unsuccessfully to bully our allies to support his ill-advised war in Iraq.

In his 2003 book, <u>Healing America</u>, Paul Simon had this to say about our being an international bully:

"A poll in Canada finds that a majority of our neighbors view us as a bully in international affairs. Polls in other nations show that even more dramatically. We do not solve that image problem—which has an impact on the cooperation we receive from other nations—simply by announcing that we are not a bully. We do it by listening to others, working with others when we can, and toning down language that is too boastful. What is true of individuals is true of nations. Others tend to see our defects more than we see our own. Those defects are much more tolerable if they are not accompanied by arrogance." (10)

A democracy like ours cannot work on the basis of a blind arrogance and patriotism.

Democracy, of, by and for the people, must leave doors open in all governmental functions and actions for public dissent and the process of correction. "To dissent", according to Thomas Jefferson (and later Senator Fulbright) "is the highest form of patriotism." Dissent is necessary and patriotic because it shows one believes his or her country is making a mistake that needs correction or can be improved.

In 1961 as he was leaving the presidency, Dwight Eisenhower warned America about the "military-industrial complex" that through its lobbying was wielding enormous power over our national government. And the military-industrial complex, having added the media to its circles, wields even greater power today! President Eisenhower also said,

> "I like to think that people in the long run are going to do more to promote peace than our governments." He goes on, and this is the crucial point: "Indeed, I think that people want peace so much that one of these days governments had better get out of the way and let them have it." (11)

The implications of these quotes are astounding.

We understand very well that dictatorships and authoritarian governments do things that are not in the best interest of their citizens, but our own democratic government? We know that the government of our great "democracy" has lied to us and misinformed us on several occasions. It is not a pleasant thought that governments themselves—even democratic governments—might be part of "the problem" in the struggle toward a more peaceful world.

The United States followed up France's failed colonial policies in Vietnam with our own failed policies. In hindsight the Vietnam War is seen to have been ill-advised in so many ways. Still another mistake was our government forcing tens of thousands of loyal Japanese-American citizens to sell their homes and businesses in a matter of days and interning them during World War II.

For decades the United States has maintained a blockade against Cuba and has bullied others to follow suit. Cuba continues to stand up against the United States and has higher levels of some measures of public health than its powerful neighbor to the north.

President G. W. Bush's second Iraq war also raises many questions about the United States instigating a preemptive war against a small country that had not directly harmed us. While our government objects strongly to other nations meddling in our affairs, especially in our elections, we have routinely meddled deeply in the affairs of other nations, especially in Latin America, including assassinating leaders of other countries in recent decades in the name of "fighting Communism". We invaded Iraq on a trumped up charge to go after "weapons of mass destruction" and no doubt because of its impressive oil reserves.

Beyond these examples involving the United States, Barbara Tuchman, in her 1984 book, The March of Folly, from Troy to Vietnam, recounts incident after incident of "boneheadedness" by national leaders in many countries through the centuries, many times to advantage the wealthy or a favored corporation. As a result of boneheaded and unjust actions by government leaders, as well as old battles and fragmentations in many parts of the world, there is a residue of old hates and animosities and border disputes, many of them centuries old. Politicians in their campaigning play on these old hatreds and injustices, but there is no way they can or ever will be rectified to the total satisfaction of the groups involved.

The principle of "self-determination" was proposed by Roosevelt and Churchill in the 1941 Atlantic Charter to deal with dismantling Europe's colonial empires after World War II. However, application of that principle has not led to the establishment of viable new nations. Yugoslavia is a case in point. The key questions are: For how small an area or population or ethnic or religious enclave should self-determination be honored? And, what resources must such an enclave have to support a viable independent nation?

In his analytical book, New Legal Foundations for Global Survival: Security Through the Security Council, Ferencz has this to say about self-determination and movements toward world government:

> "The right to self-determination does not include the right to determine that large numbers of innocent people must die to provide nationhood to every self-proclaimed ethnic entity. The right of self-defense does not include the right to render millions of people defenseless against poverty because they are condemned to an endless arms race that threatens all of humankind. Refusing to advance towards peace until there is a universal consensus on every step of the way, is to condemn the world to stand still." (12)

The best that can be hoped regarding the residue of old animosities is that members of these groups finally will accept *what is* as a starting point and that their governments will work as fairly as possible with them to reach some agreement and move ahead. Disparate groups should not waste time on old hates and disputes that can never be "put right".

Our winning the Revolutionary War while England lost is a bit like our involvement in Vietnam. However, in the latter case the roles were reversed and we played the losing role England had played during our Revolution. Our Civil War devastated both North and South and brought about a flawed reconstruction program that held the South in poverty for more than a half century. World War I was not "the war to end all wars" as it was advertised and the vindictive Versailles Treaty set the stage for World War II, a truly world-wide conflict that decimated cities and killed and wounded millions.

4. INHUMANITY TO INNOCENTS. In modern warfare most civilians have no place to flee and the international community cannot deal with masses of refugees on a continuing basis. And not even counting the hundreds of thousands of homeless from the December 2004 tsunami tragedy, for decades many thousands of refugees have lived in camps scattered around the world to which they fled to avoid death.

Palestinians for over fifty years, now third generation refugees, live in so-called "camps" that over the decades have developed into full-fledged cities of many thousands of inhabitants in the "West Bank" area. Small wonder Palestinians are bitter and have responded to Israeli tanks and aircraft (many supplied by the United States) with suicide bombers whom they see as their soldiers and their only weapon at hand. Each side seeks security, but neither can pinpoint the start of their "tit-for-tat", back and forth hostilities. In recent years the Israelis have been constructing a new "Berlin-like Wall" on Palestinian land to protect Jewish settlements from surprise attacks. Quite obviously the wall severely disrupts normal movement of Palestinians to get to their farm fields or to travel about between their villages. A UN resolution instructed Israel to stop construction of the wall, but construction continues and neither side has found security.

As it was in Lexington and Concord in April 1775 and in Vietnam, our over-whelming high-tech military force in Afghanistan and Iraq cannot cope with guerilla attacks from people inflamed as they struggle—with help from their friends—to oust still another invader from their homeland. Most of the "insurgents" in Iraq must be citizens who are acting or supporting those trying to oust an unwelcome invader.

During the first Iraq War in the early 1990s the United States used napalm and depleted uranium projectiles that spread radioactive dust. A decade of "sanctions" followed that brief war during which medical supplies and food were denied delivery, and a million Iraqis died, mostly children. These also were years during which our Gulf War veterans who had been involved with depleted uranium projectiles were experiencing the "Gulf War syndrome", and many thousands of Iraqis must have experienced the same.

Is it only barbaric if captives are beheaded and their mutilated bodies displayed? Is it barbaric only if large numbers of innocents are slaughtered, as in Germany's Holocaust or in Rwanda or Sudan's Darfur? Was it not also barbaric that a half million Iraqi children died during the 1990s for lack of food and medical care because of the United States sanctions against their government, while we mourned only our small number of lost soldiers? It is no surprise our troops were not welcomed with flowers when we invaded!

People the world over were aghast in the spring of 2004 when photos of Iraqi prisoner abuse by American forces at Abu Ghraib prison came to light. Prisoner abuse also was reported at our Guantanamo prison in Cuba. The abuses were known to the military and "investigations had been underway" for months. Would the abuses or significant reports ever have reached the public without the dramatic and damning photos? I doubt it. And will those really responsible for those policies ever be brought to justice? Time will tell.

We know there were prisoner abuses by Americans in Vietnam and in World War II. The killings, terrorism and destruction carried on by the "contra" mercenaries, supported by the Reagan administration in Nicaragua in the mid-1980s, are well known around the world. Some of the Reagan administration's illegal acts resulted in felony convictions of individuals close to the President. Several of these convictions were set aside by the first President Bush as he was leaving office. And interestingly, some of these same pardoned individuals have key posts in the G. W. Bush administration. These are some of the things that people in other countries remember very well that most Americans have forgotten or ignore.

5. WAR IS NOT NATURAL FOR HUMANS. Why have we accepted the notion that war is natural to humans? As Schmookler noted, humans attacking others and those being attacked have taken on violent means for so long that war and violence are viewed as "normal". History is written largely by the winners. History books generally carry battle stories from the "winner's" point of view, and the winner will naturally justify everything that was done to win the war. Bad things they did are ignored or given a "spin" to justify them.

Textbooks go on and on about wars and the brilliance of leaders who helped win them. That is what is taught to children, over and over, reinforced by hype from government and the media. That is the knowledge citizens of every country carry with them all their lives. Governments also build massive tourist-attracting monuments in memory of their fallen soldiers, military victories, kings and presidents. And citizens flock to them to remember their fallen fathers, sons, mothers, daughters, friends and others.

Teaching about battles and leaders generates and maintains loyalty and patriotism to that nation. Loyalty and nationalist fervor are maintained so citizens will accept sacrifice in the event of another war or to divert attention from mounting problems at home. It is a self-fulfilling process that goes on and on. However, a flag-waving "pledge of allegiance" spirit does little to develop a fair, balanced understanding of other countries and what must be done to solve domestic or global problems.

On the one hand Americans insist we are a peaceful nation and encourage democracy around the world. But on the other hand consider the following: For decades the United States government supported dictators (Batiste in Cuba, Somoza in Nicaragua, Saddam Hussein in Iraq, Trujillo in the Dominican Republic, Marcos in the Philippines, Pinoche in Chile, the Shah in Iran and others) when it suited "our interests". We even backed dictators when reform movements by the people were struggling to improve conditions in these countries. The United States CIA helped eliminate popular elected leaders who were thought to be too liberal: Mohammed Mossadegh in Iran in 1953, Salvador Allende in Chile in 1970, and President Reagan's efforts through the 1980s to oust Daniel Ortega in Nicaragua. Too often we have supported authoritarian regimes to protect the interests of American corporations, though the official justification was to "protect us from Communism". The Internet tells us what President Roosevelt apparently said about Somoza, Nicaragua's dictator for decades, "He may be a sonofabitch, but he's our sonofabitch."

How can we be "for democracy" when we ignore movements of people seeking democratic reforms? How can we be for democracy and peace and justice when we deal with brutal dictators routinely and spread military weapons around the world? The answer lies in a disconnect between our country's ideals and our pandering to the military and corporate greed. With large contributions to political candidates, our major corporations and especially our military industries have a heavy hand in that disconnect. In recent decades our media industry itself has become a part of the "military-industrial complex" about which President Eisenhower warned us. And so I repeat: For its health, a democracy depends desperately on a truly "fair and balanced" media, in all its forms.

When the Soviet Union went bankrupt and collapsed in 1990, military leaders in the United States were fearful that the Pentagon budget would be sharply reduced and that many of our country's domestic needs would be funded by the "peace dividend". However, the "peace dividend" never happened because a new enemy was found and our war machine continued to be well oiled. Jeffrey Denny, writing in Common Cause in 1992 considered why Congress was unlikely to slash the military budget:

> "The military budget has not only become a New Deal-style jobs program—albeit one that builds things the nation doesn't need— but also a powerful nexus of political, financial and ideological forces *(Eisenhower's 'military-industrial complex')* that continues to ensure billions of dollars for questionable weapon systems." (13) (*italics* by D.E.C.)

For a few years our alarm at "rogue states" was used to justify large military expenditures, and the first Bush war in Iraq justified high military spending because of the possibility of having to fight simultaneous wars in two different parts of the world at the same time. However, it was the 9/11 and other terrorist attacks that brought us the "new enemy" and pushed military spending to new highs. These events were fortuitous for President George Bush, whose new administration was foundering in the months before September 11, 2001.

War is the last chapter in failed diplomacy. War is the culmination of a process that builds with increases in a country's "defense capabilities". As adversary nations build their forces (always because their "enemy" is doing so) the chances for a triggering incident, either real or invented, magnify at each increase. The military can always find a large or small enemy to justify their budget requests and their jobs or, at the behest of government leaders, to divert attention from domestic problems.

The militarization competition and its constant demands on national budgets is an insidious problem in every government. In every government's budget the military competes with all other needs on which a civilized people should expect funding from their governments: schools, hospitals and clinics, unemployment insurance, roads and bridges, utilities, and even parks. And it must be acknowledged that each and all of these are as important to the "strength and security" of a nation as military might has been in the past. However all of these vital services take a back seat when the demands of the military are presented by politicians and couched in terms of "national security" and to "protect the homeland".

In recent decades under both Democratic and Republican presidents, America has become increasingly militarized, bellicose and polarized. With increased militarization and secrecy America is slipping into adopting a "garrison state" mentality that seriously jeopardizes our democracy.

United States citizens are being manipulated like puppets on a string by our fixation with the business-dominated media and the daily "news" from Washington....The ongoing fear of "terrorists" among us....The fear of an imminent attack of an unknown kind at an unknowable place by persons unknown....The fear when "Homeland Security" raises the country-wide terrorist danger level to orange. Whether anything of significance is happening or not, the stories released each day by the White House set the tone of concern and the level of fear with which citizens must deal as we try to get on with our daily lives.

And for its part, the corporate dominated media, by hyping stories of celebrity trials, unfortunate confrontations of family members over an unfortunate woman in a coma, massive wildfires or terrorist attacks, diverts public attention from critical issues we must face, like global warming, the need for birth control and the looming energy crisis.

6. CONCLUSION. Some may say the number of actual wars has declined in recent years. That probably is so, however, if one takes into account the civil disturbances, the seemingly endless conflict in Iraq, and the massive expenditures for everything military and the costs and disruption of "homeland security", we still live under a military cloud. It is instructive to realize that in October 2005 the United States war in Iraq will have become longer than our involvement in World War II.

Emery Reves book, <u>The Anatomy of Peace</u>, published in 1946, starts with five parallel interpretations of the years between World Wars I and II. Each account is from the viewpoint of a particular country: the United States, Great Britain, France, Germany and the Soviet Union. Each interpretation justifies everything that nation did and finds fault with the others for bringing on World War II. (14)

Reves' book became an instant best seller in Great Britain and the United States in the late 1940s and spawned discussions, town meetings and articles in many periodicals. I will have more to say about it later in this book. Reves "bottom line" is that "Peace is order based on law", or to put it more directly: to have a peaceful world we need a world structure of law that supercedes the nation, and that structure is a Limited World Government.

Albert Einstein made the same point very clearly in 1964: "Our defense is not in armaments, nor in science, nor in going underground. Our defense is in law and order." (15)

We Americans and the rest of the world are embarking on a new chapter in the history of the world, the "Age of Globalization". In recent years the corporate-dominated globalization process has been playing havoc with all aspects of how people around the world do everything. Globalization also is confusing our "patriotism". The economies of all countries have become so interdependent that, as was mentioned, the sovereignty nations held so dearly in earlier times by kings and tyrants is meaningless in today's world. The larger multinational corporations now have more power and assets than most of the world's nations and they "pledge allegiance" to no one but themselves.

But is it possible for people to gain a new larger world-embracing patriotism that would NOT eliminate loyalty to our home countries? Old allegiances need not die; they simply need to be put into a different perspective. The examples of our 13 colonies and the European Union give us hope. As we support our Constitution and our laws as the glue that holds us together as a nation, we still feel a loyalty to the state where we were born or where we live. Furthermore, we sense we can do it again on a still larger scale because we already have done it in a limited fashion with the League of Nations and the UN.

Somewhere deep within us, humans know that violence breeds violence. You simply cannot solve a problem using violent means. War and violence are simple-minded acts of power, not of reconciliation or problem solving. That is as much a fact in personal relations and the family as it is between religions or nations. A problem can be set aside for a time by violence, but that does not resolve it.

There are ways adults can solve problems without resorting to destruction and killing. We do it all the time in our daily lives. With the world having become so crowded and interdependent in so many ways, and with communication and transportation technology having developed as it has, a Limited World Government—a global system of law and order—is feasible and desperately needed now.

A new "Peace Dividend", money saved from war preparations, should be used to help people build communities and heal the world and resolve the problems that have been pushed to the sidelines for decades. This can be done only if we have a Limited World Government that could come into being from either a modified or superceded UN.

It is not easy to invent new social institutions and there will always be nay-say-ers who like things just as they are and ignore issues crying for solution. Furthermore, new institutions are rarely born perfectly able to fulfill all of the tasks that brought them into being. Witness the League of Nations and the United Nations! However, even as they were unable to "eliminate war" as their primary task, the League and the UN have done great good and still represent the human family's first significant steps on the inevitable road toward a larger patriotism and a Limited World Government.

In their 1989 book Henry Hollins, Powers and Sommers note that we live in a world struggling to get along with vast differences among us.

> "Religions, ideologies, languages, values, and political and economic institutions all vary widely between nations and within them, sup-plying abundant fuel for conflicts. These differences are too funda-mental to be ignored. But they need not be seen as innately destructive, for many of them add immeasurably to the vitality and wonder of life on this small planet. The conflicts resulting from these differences cannot magically be made to disappear, but they can be managed in such ways that resorting to force to settle them finally becomes an unnecessary and unacceptable option." (16)

For a community of adults, for a community of nations, the violence, destruc-tion and killing that all wars entail are against everything positive we believe in and strive for; wars do not represent civilized behavior! For our children and those who follow we must abolish war and get on with development of the world's first truly "global civilization".

It is time we paid attention to the words of President Eisenhower and many other world leaders, and seek more honorable and adult ways to manage our foreign policy—without war—and without deception!

It is in our short term and long-term self-interest as parents, as young and older people and as nations to slay the always hungry war monster, a monster we have been feeding for centuries. We must be willing to bear the cost of the changes needed to "wage peace" and organize a Limited World Government. With a strengthened or superceded UN we can address other critical issues that can only be resolved on a global scale. These are not utopian dreams. They are realistic assessments of what must be done for our children and for the human family to survive and prosper.

B. GLOBALIZATION AND "MAKING A LIVING"

It may seem odd to put "Globalization" and "Making a Living" together. One applies clearly to the day-by-day struggle of each individual and family to earn enough to fulfill their needs and desires, whereas the other, with its corporate domination of much of the world's economy, is at world scale. Even so, both relate profoundly to the well-being, or not, of everyone everywhere. Whether "Globalization" and "Making a Living" actually are successful for "the whole human family" is the second major problem facing this generation.

"Economic colonialism" or "corporate globalization" is the domination of the world's economy by the United States, a few other countries and a few dozen multi-national corporations. If little or nothing is done, these corporations, operating in a world of virtual international anarchy, will tighten their domination and become even more powerful. Already they are more powerful than most governments and can force their terms on poor countries struggling to "develop".

As already described, the split between rich and poor is becoming even more pronounced at all levels between individuals within countries, and between TA and TLA countries. If nothing is done the problems of individuals and countries struggling at the bottom of the world's economic system are likely to deepen, the pressures from "The Revolution of Rising Expectations" will become more intense, and if there are no significant changes the likelihood of more unrest and terrorist attacks will increase indefinitely.

In addition to "globalization" and "economic colonialism", many words come to mind relating to work and the universal struggle of all people to make a living. These include: income, poverty, wealth, fairness, sustainable economy, mixed economy, democracy, socialism, communism, and others. In this brief section several of these terms will be considered.

President Woodrow Wilson had this to say as an answer to the question, "Why are we here?":

> "You are not here merely to make a living. You are here to enable the world to live more amply, with greater vision, and with a finer spirit of hope and achievement. You are here to enrich the world. You impoverish yourself if you forget this errand." (17)

And, happily for all of us, many people *are* motivated in their lives to get along with others and try to leave the world a little better for their having lived.

Economies and governments have had a varied history in relation to the other. In earliest times life-supporting economic functions were closely tied in with decisions of chiefs and tribal councils on hunting ventures as well as control of trade and relations with "strangers", those outside their circle. Government involvement in the economy has continued with the step-by-step shift from tribes to nations. In colonial times kings dominated economic activity, levied taxes, gave land and special privileges to their inner circle, and gave exclusive rights to trading companies to develop trade in particular areas of the world.

In our time and before their breakup and shift toward capitalism, the Soviet Union and Communist China were extreme examples of government management of the economy. Democratic governments also are involved in economic matters through the many boards and commissions that have been put in place to regulate various economic-related activities and assure that these (supposedly) are operating for the "general welfare" and to benefit "the people". Actions and wars by the United States government through many years in regard to our energy needs provide another example of government policies and actions that relate to immediate and long term economic needs of a country.

In a democracy individual freedoms must be limited for the good of a community. For example, the legal sanctity of the home, traffic controls and laws, and laws about carrying guns come to mind. Citizens in a democracy should be as concerned about their responsibilities to the community as they are about their personal freedoms. A democracy cannot survive without a balance between individual freedoms and each citizen's responsibility and concern for the "health" of his or her community.

"Free enterprise" also is supposed to be regulated so that operations serve the "common good", however it doesn't always work out that way. On the surface it would seem that unregulated capitalism would be a natural fit with democracy since both emphasize freedom. However unlimited freedoms and unregulated capitalism are not compatible with democratic government. Businesses do not function with the same loyalty to a community as individuals. Businesses provide employment and smaller ones pay some taxes, but the "business of business" is to maximize profit on the investment of the owner or owners (shareholders). Businesses now move to the best place in the world to do that.

A democracy is strongest and most secure if all of its citizens are healthy and well educated, and if most adults participate in elections. Democracies are strongest and most secure when employment is high, when no one is "left behind" economically or socially, and when no one gains and uses wealth to twist the processes of government in their favor. Democracies are strongest when corporations are not given special favors as "people", and when the media functions to inform "the people" and is not a mouthpiece for "big business" or the government.

Woodrow Wilson's plea that each of us has a responsibility to help the world be a better place for all surely is a worthy ideal. But it falls on deaf ears of those driven to seek and amass fortunes. And at the other extreme of our economy, the idea of making the world a better place can't be taken seriously by the many who are struggling to survive each day with two or more jobs (or none) with little hope for even a small piece of the American Dream. Perhaps the "American Dream" is a dream of "middle class" status, but with all persons having a realistic hope of attaining that dream.

1. COMPARATIVE MEASURES OF WELL-BEING. Nations use a combination of statistics to measure their "Gross Domestic Product" (GDP). The GDP is used to compare a nation's "productivity" from year to year and in comparison with other nations that use similar measures. The GDP includes the value of all goods produced and services, regardless of why these services and materials are needed. Thus the GDP includes both the good and the bad. Note that the more auto accidents, the more sickness and medical expenses, the more litigation about anything, the more fire losses a country has, the higher is its GDP. Each of these bad events involves "goods and services" to try to put matters right, and each adds to the GDP.

However, the GDP tells us very little about how the people actually are doing or how they feel about how they are doing. More telling about human satisfaction is an index included in the UN Human Development Report. The "Human Development Index" combines information on longevity, education, and spendable income and provides a direct insight into quality of life. The August 2004 UN Human Development Report criticized foreign aid programs which do not address such issues as poverty, environmental degradation, drug trafficking and family planning. Also, and "For the fourth year in a row, a United Nations study (UN Human Development Report) has ranked Norway as the best place in the world to live." The United States ranked eighth, while African nations remained at the bottom of the list. (18)

Going beyond the UN Human Development Index, many different kinds of data might be used to derive a "Level of Personal Satisfaction" (LPS) quotient. These could include divorce, crime and suicide rates, use of tranquilizers and depression medications, unemployment rates, tobacco and alcohol consumption per capita, lottery receipts, escapist recreation use rates, and dollars paid to marriage and psychological counselors. Public data surely is available for most of these factors. Considering these factors, the LPS of individuals in TA countries is likely to indicate "less satisfaction" than in TLA countries.

Perhaps it is useless to compare countries when all are different and may be different in their statistics-gathering. By GDP levels, the level of living in Europe is about one-third less than in the United States, but travelers see little difference. Our GDP may be higher, but that includes our litigious society, our higher medical costs, our high crime and imprisonment rates, etc. On the other extreme, people in many TLA countries live on incomes of a dollar or two a day and therefore have virtually no tax base to provide schools, clinics and infrastructure.

Considering the size of the United States and its large and diverse population, our country compares reasonably with other TA countries in GDP and in average annual income of individuals and families. But millions among us have not been able to climb to the first rung of the American Dream's ladder. Our high average annual income (among the nations of the world) masks the great range of the income of Americans.

An August 2004 Associated Press release reports that nearly 36 million Americans live in poverty, and this number is steadily increasing. More ominous for our future, however, are the almost 13 million children living in poverty, almost a million more than in 1993. The report also noted that 45 million Americans have no health care insurance and must get medical care when their need becomes critical at expensive hospital emergency rooms. This puts a heavy burden on our nation's health care providers and increases premiums for those who have health insurance.

In 1937 President Franklin Roosevelt said,

> "The test of our progress isn't whether we add more to the abundance of those who have much; it is whether we provide enough for those who have too little." (19)

The question then follows: How many of our citizens are "successful" and how many have been left behind in their quest for the American Dream? A look at poverty rates in the United States shows clearly how many of us are *not* successful.

In 2001 over twelve per cent of Americans had incomes below the "poverty" line, an increase of one percentage point since 2000. In 2002 "poverty" was defined as an income below $18,100 for a family of four. One in every eight Americans living in poverty is not a pretty image for this wealthy nation to present to the world—or to ourselves!

This "one in eight in poverty" fact becomes more negatively emphatic when other factors on income distribution in our country are acknowledged. For example, the top one-percent of our adult citizens own fourteen-percent of the nation's wealth, while the bottom twenty-percent own only three-percent. This is an unreasonable and unfair balance in a "democracy" that is seeking "security" and some level of "equity"! Sales taxes add even more of a tax burden on lower income folks, proportionate to their income.

American corporate executive officers (CEOs) have the most wildly high "salaries" (along with other forms of remuneration) of any in the world. And the same can be said for our TV personalities, other entertainers, actors, actresses, and professional athletes, many of whom have incomes of millions of dollars a year. It is hard to imagine that adults playing a game or entertaining the public would have such generous incomes. But so it is. "Talking heads" on TV and other entertainers have incomes far greater than members of Congress or the President. It is exemplary that some CEOs, actors, actresses and athletes use part of their wealth for social causes or for those less well off.

In Europe and Japan corporate heads receive salaries that are less than fifty times the salary of an average worker in their factories. Estimated earnings of many heads of American corporations have skyrocketed to rates several hundred times that of one of their average workers. And it is not that American CEOs are more successful in leading their corporations. No, indeed. Wildly high salaries of American CEOs and "golden parachutes" on retirement are awarded whether their corporations make good profits, are going bankrupt and have dissipated pension funds of the workers, or have had their books "cooked".

Are these high salaries for CEOs or the others mentioned fair? That question is seldom asked in our "democracy". Many would answer that things should be left as is because competition and "what the market will pay" are at the heart of our economic system. A more useful question might be: Are obscenely high salaries for CEOs or any citizen healthy for a democracy?

Obscenely high salaries have serious long-term negative consequences for the health of a democracy. Exorbitant salaries create a new elite whose wealth can be used for a lavish life style, but more critical to the health of our democracy, to influence election campaigns. This wealth is passed on to later generations and the cycle of influencing political action through wealth can continue for several generations. The basic concept of "one person—one vote" goes out the window. Campaign Finance Reform, inheritance-limiting laws and less wildly ranging incomes are a "must" if we are to have a healthy democracy "of, by and for the people".

Also, our "one person one vote" concept also is distorted in the United States by corporations having been given, by error, legal status as persons. I will have more to say about that and about taxes in the next section.

2. TAXES IN THE UNITED STATES. What do taxes in the United States have to do with "Healing the World"? Taxes obviously have to do with the wealth of a country. How a country spends its tax revenue can have international repercussions. Witness the Iraq war that is using each week more than $1 billion of tax revenue from United States citizens! Taxes also are closely related to "making a living", a hot topic always but especially during election years. No politician in any country wants to raise taxes. Yet our civilized way of life is based on citizens paying taxes to governments to provide many important services that citizens can't efficiently provide for themselves.

The tax system in the United States is not set up for fairness to low and middle income individuals and families. Sales taxes and the lure of state supported lotteries and gambling boats disadvantage the poor, proportionate to their lower incomes. Income taxes in the United States are based on a "progressive tax" system that has a sliding scale of rates with higher rates applying as one's income rises. Thus, the wealthiest pay the highest rates and those with the lowest incomes pay the lowest rate, if any. However, the highest of our "progressive" tax rates are significantly lower than those in other TA nations, and loopholes in United States tax laws still permit accumulation of vast wealth at the upper levels, and, indeed, many high income individuals and corporations contrive to pay little or no income tax at all.

Progressive taxing helps carry out FDR's suggestion that a measure of a nation's progress is how it treats the least advantaged of its citizens. But can higher taxes for those with higher incomes be fair in a democracy? The simple logic and justification for higher income taxes for the wealthy is that, in addition to individual efforts, it is the economic and governmental systems and tax rates of a country that make higher incomes and wealth accumulation possible. The wealthy therefore should pay a higher tax to protect and maintain a system that made possible their higher income. Furthermore, they have more to lose if our system does not work and should therefore be willing to pay more to keep it running as it is. A final point is that using the tax revenue from the wealthy to help those less well off can help maintain political stability. For their prosperity and their security, democracies must depend on stability and an "informed electorate" to make wise decisions for their country's future.

Another problem with our tax system is that its rules are complicated and by loopholes and staffs of lawyers, many corporations and high income individuals pay little if any income tax at all. This is not fair and needs to be fixed. A loophole in the tax code even allows an individual or corporation to be advantaged by establishing a "residence" or "main office" "off shore". With attention to international financial transactions, a global government could help control this kind of "tax dodge" problem.

State sponsored lotteries and gambling boats are an ill-advised method employed by states to gain revenue in recent decades. Gambling ventures draw much of their revenue from those least able to pay in the vain hope of a windfall that could propel them from their meager state. Thus, state sponsored gambling functions as a hidden tax on the poor. Further, gambling has the possible consequence of gambling addiction. Studies have shown that increased costs for gambling-related social services far outweigh the "cut" states receive from gambling operations.

Still another problem with our tax and economic system that relates to the rest of the world is the manner by which our corporations have come to be accepted as "persons". Since 1886 corporations have been treated in our courts as "persons" in terms of their rights. This has been continued for well over a century even though it came about as a legal recording mistake. Corporations never actually were given that "personhood" designation by any court action or decision. This legal mistake happened as a result of a simple recording error in a Supreme Court case that the courts have not corrected. (20) The mistake continues simply as "legal precedent".

Congress should rectify this erroneous practice of treating United States corporations as persons. Corporations are not people, all corporate decisions and actions are made *by people*. Further, "corporations" can't vote, even though they make major contributions to sway elections and gain access to our legislative halls at all levels.

With campaign contributions especially from all kinds of corporations and the wealthy, Pork-barrel politics and special interest financing of the United States government has become so prevalent and powerful that some say we have a "corporatocracy" rather than a "democracy"!

Here is a simple idea that might help us and our democracy: We put limitations on who can drive a vehicle and who can vote. Perhaps the privilege of making campaign contributions should be limited to those who can vote, thereby curtailing contributions from corporations! Making this change could help the American people regain control of the electoral process! Such a step also would help control corporate globalization.

3. GLOBALIZATION. This "Age of Globalization" is coming on like a juggernaut and is playing havoc with all aspects of how people around the world do everything. The key question about globalization is not "How can we stop it"? The key question is: "Can globalization be controlled so it will help "the people" rather than simply enrich CEOs and shareholders in multi-national corporations?" My short answer to that second question is, "Yes", but it can be done only through a Limited World Government!

Globalization is not the first economic system that has brought on profound changes in how the world does business. There have been massive changes in how people "make a living" before in the human saga on Earth, but those shifts usually took centuries to mature and spread. Examples are the 7000 years ago shift from a hunting and gathering way of life in the Middle East to a settled agriculture-based life that spread to most parts of the Earth. The shift in Europe from the feudal to a mercantile system in the sixteenth to eighteenth centuries is another example, as is the eighteenth and nineteenth century Industrial Revolution, a revolution many TLA countries—a century and a half later—are still struggling to adopt.

But it took centuries for these earlier "new" modes of economic activity to mature and spread around the world and make a difference in the lives of most people. Things have speeded up in our time, making globalization different from all earlier eras of major change. We now live in a world where changes come on at an astonishing speed.

We can cite those three earlier economic revolutions, but we also have to acknowledge that the "Electronic Communications Revolution" involving computers, fax, email and the Internet have had a lot to do with making corporate globalization process possible. "Globalization" could not have advanced so quickly without easy high speed transfer of massive amounts of data by fiber-optic cable, easy around the world communication by phone, FAX and Internet, and rapid transcontinental air travel of key corporate personnel.

In the old days of colonies and colonial rule, businesses in the "mother country" in Europe developed basic resources in each colony that were needed by industries and people back home. Colonies were restricted or discouraged from doing any manufacturing themselves. Through the centuries of Europe-dominated colonialism and up until World War II many colonies developed export economies based on one or two agricultural or mineral export commodities, with the colony having no control of the price of those commodities. And the colonies were forced to import "finished" goods from the "mother country".

England's forcing the American colonies to import finished goods from England and prohibiting the colonies from establishing factories of their own was one of the causes of our revolution. And Mahatma Gandhi's famous "March to the Sea" to encourage Indians to make their own salt from sea water (which led finally to India's independence) was done to oppose Great Britain's efforts to force India to import salt from Britain.

Since its birth in recent decades globalization has been a manifestation of major multi-national corporations from TA countries (most of them from the United States). "Corporate Globalization" now dominates the world and has more power than the UN. Large multinational corporations seek to lower their costs and increase their profits by building factories and using low cost laborers overseas to perform some of their service operations, to manufacture goods from local agricultural or mineral raw materials or to assemble finished goods from imported parts. TLA countries have unorganized laborers who will work for a fraction of the cost of American or European workers. And the wealthy elite and the new small middle class in TLA countries have become markets for finished goods and more specialized manufactures from TA nations.

"Corporate Globalization" and the current situation in the world amount to a new kind of "colonialism". We could call it "economic colonialism". A "mother country" no longer actually operates the government of a TLA "developing" country and directs economic development for the direct benefit of the "mother country". Instead, and just as insidiously, major corporations and a TA country, operating in part through the World Bank and the International Monetary Fund, meddle in the TLA country's government and make many demands. Such demands may include stifling people's movements, dismantling social programs, and making changes in laws relating to trade, investment and production. Such demands benefit the corporations and the dominating country, rather than the developing country or most of its people.

Nicaragua's case, mentioned earlier, is an excellent example of how a powerful country can dominate a smaller one politically and economically. With the United States looking on the Somoza family dictatorially dominated the country from 1937 to 1979, when they were dislodged by a popular revolt. President Ortega and his Nicaraguan Sandinista Party won election overwhelmingly in 1984 and developed exceptional programs in local health care and education that were applauded by the UN. They also were taking on land reform, to put into the hands of small Nicaraguan farmers land that was idle and in the hands of absentee owners. Besides building schools and clinics, President Ortega also wanted to establish in Nicaragua a "mixed economy", to include some government-owned and operated basic economic activities, leaving the rest to be "free market".

President Ortega also did not want Nicaragua to be dominated by any other country. He sought help from the United States but was rebuffed, so he sought and received aid from European countries and the Soviet Union. Although Nicaragua's Communist Party was small (smaller than several European countries with whom we have had normal relations through the years), President Reagan saw President Ortega as a threat to the United States' political and economic domination of Central and South America. Reagan therefore set out to break the Sandinista Party's hold on Nicaragua so other Latin American countries would continue to look to the United States as their "big brother" and not seek relations with the Soviet Union.

Reagan's illegal terrorist activities moved forward under the bloody banner of "anti-communism". During the mid-1980s and operating out of the White House, President Reagan authorized the illegal sale of military equipment to Iran. The proceeds from these illegal sales supported activities managed from the White House under Colonel Oliver North. This operation was designed to disrupt and undermine President Ortega's Sandinista government. Mercenary terrorists (disaffected Nicaraguans and other Central Americans better known as the "contra") were successful. Ortega's Sandinista Party administration was undermined and in 1990 was defeated by a candidate openly supported by the United States.

Besides having small Communist political parties, Italy, France, and many other countries with whom we deal routinely, have mixed economies that even include government-run airlines, railroads, and health services that are managed on behalf of the people of those countries. In contrast, our President, favoring what he calls an "ownership society", would like virtually all government run services to be discontinued or sold off to private enterprises.

In our country we hear a lot about "capitalism", "market economy", "private enterprise", and "free enterprise". These terms are used in Washington and the media as if they automatically go with democracy and are as sacred in our culture as "motherhood and apple pie". This is especially true in the United States' simultaneous push for "democracy" and a "market economy" in Iraq. The explanation from the President is that service would be improved and costs reduced if private enterprises could take over services now provided by governments through fees and taxes.

We should be careful not to tie "democracy" to particular economic concepts. There can be no guarantee that private businesses, with all of their own problems with truth, efficiency, monopoly, price gouging and secrecy would provide services more fairly and efficiently than they are now provided by governments. Corporate scandals revealed through the years and graft and corruption by corporations providing services in Iraq should counter President Bush's confidence in the private sector. Capitalism does not need democracy. In fact, by its very secretive and competitive nature it seems to work best—in terms of profits for owners and shareholders—when it is managed from closed boardrooms.

In a democracy the people can opt for a mixed economy or not. However, a mixed economy can work well only if board and commission members appointed by mayors, governors and the President are diligent in overseeing that government run agencies and enterprises are run efficiently on behalf of all of the people. Unfortunately things have not worked out well "for the people" in recent years because some oversight boards and commissions have become dominated by individuals from competing private enterprises. The fox has been put in charge of the chicken coop!

The record of "deregulation" of services to the public and their privatization in the United States in recent years has not been good. Prices have *not* come down and service has not been improved as promised in example after example. The saving and loan debacle; the constantly rising prices for cable TV, telephone and cell phone services, and the turning back to state management state prisons that had been privately operated are cases in point. And a number of privately operated Charter Schools are having problems delivering the educational improvements that were promised.

Another phenomenon in the operation of multinational corporations is happening on a world scale. Clothing and shoe manufacture, computer assembly, and many of America's more labor intensive industries have established factories in China, Taiwan, Korea, the Philippines, Mexico and probably elsewhere. Finished products for the United States market, even some of our military equipment, are now manufactured or assembled "overseas" and then imported to the United States. This is called "Outsourcing" and it supplies the American market with many of its manufactured products. Manufacturing jobs are lost in the United States, and, as we import far more finished products and other materials than we export, our trade deficit (our "balance of trade") is thrown farther and farther out of balance.

Our deficit is taken up by foreign governments and banks that routinely purchase United States bonds. Through most of United States history our country was a creditor nation. In recent decades we have become the world's greatest debtor nation in history! Our national debt is over SEVEN TRILLION Dollars and is increasing rapidly, largely because of the Iraq war and tax breaks for the wealthy! The financial system of the United States would be thrown into massive disarray if several major foreign creditors (China, Germany, Japan) took action to cash in their Treasury Notes and US bonds at the same time! Already in the past three years the value of the US dollar has fallen sharply against the Euro and Yen. And the end is not in sight.

Recently, "off-shore hiring" also is taking place as service jobs for records transcribing and answering services (phone banks to take care of high volume but routine calls between corporations and customers) are being shifted overseas to lower paid locals who are trained to speak with American accents. Bangalore, India, has become a center for such services, facilitated by world wide instant fiber-optics networks.

In this increasingly interdependent world, policies of the World Bank and the International Monetary Fund (IMF) constitute a serious problem to improving the lives of most people in TLA countries. A disquieting 2004 book, Confessions of an Economic Hit Man, by John Perkins, relates Perkins' experience working for corporations pushing development projects and forcing reductions in social services and safety nets from TLA governments. The policies of the World Bank and IMF and multinational corporations since World War II clearly have benefited investors and banks in the TA countries. The policies of these agencies have helped corporations that have operations in TLA countries. These policies also have helped the power brokers and educated elite in TLA countries that have received loans from the World Bank and IMF. But they have not helped the lives of most people in the TLA countries.

To qualify for a development loan World Bank and IMF policies require a TLA government to reduce public expenditures for schools and social services, open their country to foreign investment and trade, permit construction of foreign managed factories, and shift from subsistence farming to emphasize products for export. Many large dam construction projects have dislocated thousands of the common people, leaving them with little or no compensation or a way to earn a living.

Development loans, therefore, do not benefit most of the common people or lead to an improved and sustainable economy. Many TLA countries that received loans and grants in years past are deeply in debt and have been forced to renegotiate their loans more than once, with even more stringent measures required that further reduce expenditures for public services. As Emad Mekay said, "Critics of the IMF and the bank (World Bank) say the institutions have strayed from their original mandate over the past 60 years, moving toward a form of market fundamentalism that only considers the profit of Northern powers (TA nations), blind to human costs." (21)

As outsourcing, robotics and offshore hiring change the needs and skills for workers, jobs in the United States are no longer "for a lifetime", nor are they as secure as they used to be with the same enterprise. A corporation's first loyalty is to its stockholders, not its workers' paychecks or pensions or its community.

A decade ago free trade was a significant issue in the United States' presidential campaign. NAFTA (North Atlantic Free Trade Association) was a dividing issue in its prospect of joining the United States with Canada and Mexico in a free trade agreement. Trade was to flow freely among these countries, and there was supposed to be an increase in jobs, prosperity, etc.

The concept is a great one, but because it is such an uneven playing field, it hasn't worked out to the benefit of most American workers. United States environment and worker standards have been put in limbo. There have been significant job losses in many basic categories in the U.S., especially in manufacturing. Job increases have come only in federal Homeland Security and lower paying service categories. Legislation for a similar trade agreement (CAFTA—Central American Free Trade Association) is being debated in Congress, but it holds no greater promise than the NAFTA agreement.

We are in a time when, for the first time in memory, the next generation has the prospect of a lower level of living than their parents. The rich get richer and the poor get poorer and the middle class is declining as many are being pushed down. Pensions and savings are in jeopardy. Fear and stress levels are high and health care needs and costs are going off the chart.

These stresses would be greatly reduced if health care and pensions were made portable and would move with the worker. A simple (but perhaps revolutionary!) way to do this would be for all employers and employees to put their pension contributions into a secure federal pension trust fund, to be used only on behalf of workers when they retire. Besides facilitating portability, this arrangement would eliminate the danger of pension loss by mismanagement or bankruptcy. Witness the United Airlines abandoning pension obligations as they negotiated bankruptcy in May 2005.

With mounting interdependence and mixing of cultures old-fashioned patriotism, like sovereignty, is becoming less important. Whether we recognize it or not, and regardless of whatever allegiances we may have, we are all citizens of the Earth. Paul Simon quotes Midge Miller on a related point:

> "Once you are a parent you can be a good parent or a bad parent, but you can't be a non-parent. Citizenship is the same. You can be a good citizen or a bad citizen, but you can't be a non-citizen". (22)

Using the same reasoning, we can be a good world citizen or a bad world citizen, but we were born on Earth and therefore none of us can deny being a world citizen! As world citizens—who want the best for our children and others—we must work together to make globalization more humane and responsive to the needs of the people.

4. CONCLUSION. Can a country as rich and powerful as ours do better for the poor among us? Is there no way the poor can move up the ladder to be proud participants in the American Dream or the dream of a better life for themselves and their families? Pride and hope are two ingredients essential to a happy, productive life for any person, a family and also for a nation. But these

can come only when people know their government is working for the common people and not for special interests or a wealthy minority.

Much has been said in this section about ordinary people in many countries, including our own, who have not benefited from corporate globalization. It does not have to be that way. International activities of corporations can and must be managed "for the people"!

The great challenge and opportunity for our time is to gain control of the globalization process so it may benefit virtually all the world's people. The globalization process is so new that opportunities are now open to intervene and direct the globalization process for the betterment of humanity.

But how? What agency can monitor or control powerful multi-national corporations? At present there is no such agency in the world. The UN has no way of doing it. There is no relevant international law to deal with the issues. The economic power multi-national corporations wield in their home countries will make it difficult to force them to be more humane in the world.

How, then, can we ever hope to rein in such powerful players on the international scene? How can we hope to control powerful players that are taking advantage of the anarchy that now exists among nations? The only answer to these "How" questions is through a Limited World Government that has certain functions and is strong enough to fulfill them. Just how a new global institution like a Limited World Government might control multi-national corporations and render them to be more humane is presented in Part III.

C. THE EARTH AND PEOPLE

GEOGRAPHY LESSON

There is but one world…
    And yet…
    There are countless worlds…
    A unique world in the mind
        of each of Earth's creatures.

There are four oceans…
    And yet…
    There is but one world-ocean
    And unnumbered lakes and seas
        that bathe the shores
        of all the lands.

There are five continents…
    With many nations
    And countless ethnic groups,
    Each guarding its heritage…
    And yet…
        we are one human family
        who depend on our Earth home
          and each other
          for our brief walk in the sun
          and for our daily bread.

But there is ignorance,
    And there is greed and arrogance,
    As man thinks he owns the Earth
    And can do as he pleases…
    And yet, in truth, it is the reverse.

> In its persistent
>> And not always gentle manner,
>> The Earth owns man.

David E. Christensen
December 30, 1974

My poem is one perspective about the Earth and its human family. Here is another.

We are diverse. As organisms we are fragile. We carry thousands of years of cultural baggage. And whether we fully understand it or not, in addition to our needs for food, water, shelter, air and hope, we occupy a very narrow environmental niche in terms of temperature ranges, precipitation and solar energy. We depend desperately on our Earth's finely tuned systems for survival.

Seventy-two per cent of the Earth is covered by the salt water oceans. Humans have had a devastating effect on fish and other life forms in these waters. Many of the larger life forms are in danger of extinction and large areas of coastal waters have become so polluted that marine life has been sorely disrupted. Even so, the vast oceans themselves with their currents, their depths and deposits of silt, sand, minerals and numerous sunken small and large ships are still pretty much as they have been through the ages.

So that leaves about one-fourth of the Earth that is "land". Humans have had little effect on most mountain, desert and sub-arctic forest areas which account for half of the land area. So it comes down to only about one-half of the land or one-eighth of the Earth's surface on which humans have had their greatest effect and on which we depend most.

Consider also that most human effects have been on Earth's skin, to a depth of only a few dozen feet. Humans have drilled holes over a mile deep in search of oil and water here and there and have been successful enough to make the searching worth the effort. We also have dug large and deep holes here and there for minerals, and some areas look like moonscapes for our digging! However, our major changes have been to clear forests and native grasses for farming and to modify the drainage of that land. And we have done much more changing or paving over the three per cent of the land surface (and near surface) that has been converted to cities, roads, airports, subways and other urban-related uses.

Even though human changes have involved such a limited portion of the Earth, those effects have been profound. They are especially profound when we realize we have changed most the portion of the Earth on which we humans depend the most: our farmlands and cities. We need also to add the atmosphere to the equation. The human effect on the atmosphere has been overwhelming with our intense use of fossil fuels. And, with global warming, we are slowly learning, to our dismay, the consequences of that use.

1. RENEWABLE RESOURCES. For at least 150 years "prophets" have admonished humans on how we are misusing our Earth home, and each "prophet" expressed warnings and misgivings about the future of the human race. George Marsh, W. C. Lowdermilk, Fairfield Osborn, William Vogt, Paul Sears, Karl Sax, Vernon Gill Carter, Tom Dale, Georg Borgstrom, Alvin Toffler, Stewart Udall, Lester Brown, and former Vice President Al Gore are among these.

In 1867 George Marsh wrote "The Earth as Modified by Human Action". (23) Despite its well documented message of how mankind has degraded the Earth, it was largely ignored by a nation that was "feeling its oats" in expansion to the Pacific West Coast and in its fixation on the bourgeoning Industrial Revolution. Marsh's book was ignored until the drought and massive dust storms hit our Midwest during the early years of Franklin Roosevelt's presidency in the 1930s. The lengthy drought and massive dust storms in the midst of the depression got the attention of the public and the president, and the federal government took action.

In the late 1930s W. C. Lowdermilk, an assistant chief of the U.S. Soil Conservation Service in the Department of Agriculture, made an extended trip of Western Europe, North Africa and the Middle East to study soil erosion and land use issues. When he returned he wrote and spoke about the spread of deserts throughout the region. He also wrote about the impending disaster that faced our country if we did nothing about our losses of soil by erosion and ill-advised farming techniques. His booklet, "Conquest of the Land Through 7,000 Years" paints a sorry story of empire after empire declining as they misused their lands over the years. (24)

William Vogt carried on Lowdermilk's concern when Vogt wrote <u>Road to Survival</u> in 1948:

"Because of the great abundance of the earth's resources we have taken them for granted. But now, over most of the globe, as this (Vogt's) book shows, we are face to face with a serious depletion of 'resource capital'. More than one country is already bankrupt. Such bankruptcy has wiped out civilizations in the past; there is no reason for thinking we can escape the same fate, unless we change our ways." (25)

Over a half-century later and continuing Lowdermilk's and Vogt's concern, a 2004 UN report documents the rapid expansion of deserts in many parts of our Earth. The UN report informs us that

> "Slash and burn agriculture, sloppy conservation, overtaxed water supplies and soaring populations are mostly to blame. But global warming is taking its toll, too." The report goes on, "By 2025, two-thirds of arable (farmable) land in Africa will disappear, along with one-third of Asia's and one-fifth of South America's....135 million people....are at risk of being displaced. (26)

Such an ominous prediction of loss of arable land in Africa, Asia and Latin America in the two decades ahead! And such a calamity, not only for the 135 million people who may be displaced, but also for billions of others unless action is taken soon to deal with global warming, population control and farming techniques. Darfur and Uganda are merely the tip of the iceberg.

Especially since the Industrial Revolution in the mid and late 1800s, a rapidly enlarging human family has pressed harder and harder on the Earth for sustenance. We have used the Earth's bounty beyond its ability to repair itself. Air and water pollution and global warming are real threats to our future. We are clearing rainforests in Central and South America to raise cattle and soybeans, thereby reducing the Earth's ability to maintain adequate oxygen levels in the atmosphere. We are fast using up many of the Earth's "one-time-use" resources, like petroleum. (There is more about that in the next section.) In too many areas fresh water has become a precious, limited resource. We desperately need to develop a balance between what our Earth offers on the one hand and how the many humans are to be supported on the other.

The Earth offers much and has its limits on what is available, and that is it! Humans cannot "negotiate" with the Earth to achieve the necessary balance. Developing a sustainable balance between what the Earth offers and can maintain and the demands of the human population depends entirely upon what humans do. We humans CAN do something about how we use the Earth. And we CAN do something about the rapid rise in the number of humans who draw on the Earth's resources. It is up to us, in our capacity to think and plan, to work out a long-range sustainable balance between the Earth and its human population.

Paul Simon called for action to

"make this tough but destructible place called earth a safe and healthy place for future generations." He goes on: "That will require greater cooperation with other nations. Air and water pollution do not recognize national boundaries. Poorer nations cannot be expected overnight to meet the standards that industrial nations set for themselves. The Kyoto agreement on earth-warming gives developing nations more time to meet the standards we have—and it should. Cairo, Egypt, has visibly weaker air pollution requirements that the U.S. has, but the Egyptian per capita income level makes it impossible for that nation to meet rigid standards overnight. Two reports say that Beijing's air is 'sixteen times dirtier than in New York and....thirty-five times more contaminated than in London.' Should they take steps to do something about this? Yes. Their dirty air ultimately hurts us. Can we expect them to move as fast as we could on such problems? No. Our industrialization took place over a century during which pollution went unchecked. Theirs is taking only a few decades as they struggle to join the modern world." (27)

A Bible quotation ignores the responsibility of humans to maintain the Earth for future generations. Genesis, 1. 28 says: "Be fruitful, and multiply, and replenish the earth, and subdue it, and have dominion over the fish of the sea and over the foul of the air and over every living thing that moveth upon the earth." The verse clearly instructs humans to dominate the earth and take it over for human purposes. Humans thoughtlessly have adopted this "hubris" approach for thousands of years as our numbers have increased from a few millions to over six billion. And empire after empire has come and gone.

Especially over the last two thousand years humans have dominated the Earth. During those millennia we have selected resources to be used, domesticated selected plants and animals and destroyed lands and species in the process. In blind efforts to sustain ourselves as we increase in numbers, humans have had and are having effects on the Earth's surface as powerful as geologic and biologic forces have had through the ages.

Despite our impressive technology, we humans are also part of the natural environment. We are a species of animals, the most advanced in some ways. And, like all living things, we depend on other living things for food. We need to remember this as we work to develop a balanced and sustainable relationship with the Earth.

Man on the Landscape by Vernon Gill Carter begins with an intriguing observation. He notes that a few thousand years ago there would have been very little air pollution, rivers usually would have run clear, and nature could repair itself from damage by storm, catastrophe or the small number of humans. Carter then notes that air and water pollution, soil erosion and depletion and the way cities completely remake the living environments for so many of us are all "abnormal" in nature. However, they have been with us for so long that, like war, we accept them as "normal". (28)

For many decades during the eighteenth and nineteenth centuries agricultural research and the development of agricultural machines made it appear there was no end to increases in agricultural productivity. However, a few decades ago it appeared that increasing yields for major crops was at a dead end. As was mentioned, the "Green Revolution" came along in the 1970s based on genetic research and the use of fertilizers. But its advantages were limited to new wheat and rice varieties.

No research breakthroughs for other crops have brought similar results. Only a small portion of farmers were able to take advantage of the Green Revolution. However, over the decades, with increasing costs of seed and fertilizer and water pollution from run-off, the Green Revolution's promise has dimmed. Farmers and regions that built a way of life around Green Revolution technologies are in difficulty.

Although controversial, in recent decades agricultural biotechnology offers new hope of increasing productivity of basic crops in diverse environments around the world. That is welcome news in a world that is adding about 80 million new mouths to feed each year. However, as with earlier breakthroughs, who can know how long biotechnology-based advances in food production might last or their long term effects on humans?

For centuries ingenious methods for pulling water from rivers and irrigating from reservoirs have helped farmers in many parts of the world to produce crops from areas otherwise too dry for farming. It also has helped farmers to increase yields in areas of adequate precipitation by reducing one element in the gamble of farming. Thus, especially for the last sixty years "supplementary irrigation" has brought large areas, such as the United States semi-dry plains states, into more intensive production of basic crops.

Over hundreds of years "Nature" has slowly recharged underground water-storing rocks in the Great Plains "Ogallala Aquifer" by slow seepage from the Rocky Mountains. But more and more water is being drawn from this source. Already wells are being dug deeper and deeper and stronger pumps must be used. In not too many years the region may have to revert to pasture land and raising livestock, just as it was in the "Old West" days of our country. And surplus population will have to leave or find other ways to support themselves.

This example of overuse of ground water in the United States Midwest can be replicated in different ways throughout the world. In parts of California's great Central Valley the ground level actually settled several feet after ground water was withdrawn from aquifers deep below the surface, thus ruining forever these porous rocks from any future recharging.

Everywhere there is competition for the Earth's limited supply of fresh water. As Arundhati Roy documents in India, private companies are getting into the act in many places, and when they do the common people are at the mercy of these for-profit businesses for one of their absolute necessities. This water issue was one of Paul Simon's concerns. It is a critical issue because, like food and shelter, fresh water is an essential for life. Access to fresh water should be acknowledged as a "right".

Fresh water comprises only about one per cent of the world's total water supply, the rest is salty ocean water. And much of the fresh water is locked up in ice caps and glaciers. Desalinization of ocean water is possible and is used in several very dry coastal areas in the world like Kuwait and Israel. However at present it is too expensive for general use or to mitigate the world's pending fresh water problem.

Just as most of the Earth's surface is covered with salt water, most of the land is not suitable for raising crops. In fact, only about one-fourth of the land area or one-sixteenth of the Earth's surface is "arable", that is, suitable for raising crops. The rest of the useable half of the Earth's land area is in permanent pasture and forest. The remaining half of the Earth's land area is in desert, non-productive arctic forests and high mountains.

Arable land is a "renewable resource", as also are forest areas, natural grassland, and even underground water resources if the structure of the aquifer is not destroyed. Humans are fortunate that both fresh water and soil are "renewable resources". That is, if managed wisely and not overused they can be renewed and produce forever. However, if we don't use them wisely—as in the case of erosion or crushed aquifers—they can be destroyed. As the writings of

Lowdermilk, Vogt, others and the UN report have informed us, over the centuries too many of the Earth's arable and pasture lands have been used poorly and turned into deserts. And it is happening today on a large scale in Africa.

Even if the population growth rate can be reduced or brought to zero or lower, we still must take whatever actions are needed to assure that our water supplies and arable land are maintained, because these are the basic support of our food supply now and forever. Part of the solution to our "food for the future" problem must come from protection and maintenance of our arable lands, but also in decreasing wastage of food, reducing loss of food by rodents, reducing food consumption by individuals (which will help the obesity problem) and, as we have repeated, in reducing the human birth rate!

Besides using our renewable resources wisely, we also must protect the rest of the Earth's natural environment. Why? So much of what happens to the renewable resources depends on precipitation and water flowing from mountains, forests and grasslands. Maintaining these natural areas is as important as maintaining arable lands! Furthermore, we must protect all forms of living things in all of these areas not only because it is right to do so, but as a genetic pool for possible uses in the future.

Two war-related tragedies also relate to the decrease in our world supply of productive land and they also randomly destroy people. These are:1. The horror of landmines left long after hostilities have ceased in an area, and 2. The environmental calamity of the United States' arrogant use of radioactive depleted uranium. This material is used to harden the projectiles of bombs and missiles so they can penetrate tanks and buildings. Despite its name, "depleted uranium" is far from harmless; it is still radioactive!

During war times many land mines and radioactive-tipped bombs and missiles were used in arable land areas. Thus, besides killing or maiming soldiers (including our own) and innocent people long after hostilities have ceased, old battlefields remain non-productive "no man's land" for years. Abandoned landmines do their random damage to innocents including children over decades. Radioactive dust from depleted uranium bombs and missiles, like the fallout from our Hiroshima and Nagasaki bombs that ended World War II, will remain a life threatening hazard to humans and other creatures for thousands of years wherever these weapons have been used.

2. FOSSIL FUELS AND OTHER RESOURCES. Besides the renewable resources of land and fresh water (and air!), humans obviously depend very heavily on other bounties of nature. The Industrial Revolution brought on a

sudden demand for "fossil fuels" (coal, petroleum and natural gas) and an enormous increase in our use of metals and natural fertilizer materials. The shift came about after wood supplies had been depleted near early industrial cities and towns, especially in England where industrial development began. In the United States the use of metals, especially steel, boomed with our making more and more "machines to make other machines", plus railroad tracks and equipment, automobiles, farm machines and the steel skeletons of tall buildings.

In 2004 Lester Brown wrote <u>Plan B: Rescuing a Planet under Stress and a Civilization in Trouble.</u> (29) In this prescient book Brown lays out scenario after scenario how all elements of our natural environment and heritage are deteriorating under the crush of more and more people and notes our apparent lack of interest in reversing these declines. He documents and explains how our cropland is shrinking, how fresh water and petroleum are becoming more scarce, and how global warming is real and will—if left unabated—wreak havoc around the world.

Brown also proposes at least a partial solution. It is simple in concept but would be difficult to apply. He proposed that the price of all goods include the costs to the environment of all processes in that product's production, transportation and use. It would apply to all kinds of production and would include advertising and administrative costs as well. Such realistic pricing would quickly help consumers know the true value and environmental cost of everything they use and might help people make more environmentally sound choices in their purchases. Even so, it would not provide the huge alternative energy source that will be needed.

Coal and petroleum are now the energy backbone of our industrialized "Western" way of life. However, unlike renewable soil and fresh water resources, coal, petroleum and gas are not renewable in nature. Coal, petroleum and gas were made millions of years ago in our Earth's history and none is being made now in nature. Instead, they are "non-renewable" or "one time use" resources.

The higher prices that came on during 2004 and 2005 are just the beginning. In only two or three decades increasing prices may put the fossil fuel resources out of reach of "one time uses" in our autos, planes and power plants. The United States and many other countries are endowed with large coal reserves that, with new technologies, could provide energy to keep our country and others "on wheels" for more decades. There also are massive oil shale reserves in Western United States (roughly half of the world's reserves according to the Internet) which can yield liquid petroleum using high tech methods. These are likely to come into use when petroleum prices have risen high enough (to $60 or $70 a barrel?) and that time may not be far off.

There is interesting research underway looking toward use of oil shale, but development of oil shale poses difficult technological and ecological problems for the environment and for protecting underground water resources. Even when oil shale may become very important in providing energy for the United States and perhaps some for export, we must recognize that, like crude oil (liquid) petroleum reserves, oil shale also is a finite one-time-use resource, and it, too, will be depleted. At best, and considering increasing needs for energy around the world, full development of oil shale would provide energy for only several decades and it would leave large areas as barren "moonscapes".

In an editorial titled, "Let's Stop Sleepwalking Through History", Stewart Udall, Secretary of the Interior from 1961 to 1969, said,

> "For the last two centuries the burning of fossil fuel—coal, natural gas and crude oil—has been propelling human civilization. But fossil fuels are finite—they really will run out—and their use has altered Earth's atmosphere. On both fronts, Americans are in denial. "Why are we so blind? We have been conditioned to believe that catastrophe will not occur, that mankind is perpetually on the threshold of discoveries that will magically solve our dilemmas." (30)

If we do not develop adequate alternative energies very soon to replace cheap gasoline and diesel fuel there will be hardship, chaos, disruption and perhaps even revolution. This will happen when all gasoline dependent countries, TA and TLA, hit the "high price wall" at about the same time with insufficient alternatives to fulfill their energy demands at prices the people can afford. All of the world's people and nations will be scrambling to do anything—even to waging futile energy wars (like our war in Iraq?)—to retain their gasoline-driven way of life. Even democracies are likely to fall victim to "leaders" who will promise anything and everything.

To seek long-term solutions, intelligent folks will ask, "What can I do to support changes needed to deal with the reality when petroleum will no longer be relatively inexpensive?" "What *can* we do immediately?" Suggestions? SUVs should be "history"—even now! Hybrid autos should be "in"! (I'm on my second one.) Carpooling and public transportation should be encouraged. Our cities should be made more compact. Spread-out suburbs should be discouraged. Bicycling should be encouraged. The best we can do with fossil fuels is to use them wisely in the most efficient vehicles, appliances, power plants and cities we can design. We must take these actions even as we develop adequate alternative energy sources for our vehicles and power plants.

Intelligent people plan ahead for themselves and their families, and nations must do the same. A generation from now, the remaining and higher priced fossil fuels will be needed and used for more specialized purposes, like pharmaceuticals, plastics, etc.

The only reasonable strategy is for governments, universities and corporations to encourage and support research on alternative energy sources during these years before we hit the petroleum "high price and depletion wall". Wind, tides, geothermal and biomass sources need continuing research and can provide some energy, but not enough. Coal and oil shale research should be well supported. Nuclear energy would be a boon if it could be generated without building up stores of dangerously radioactive waste materials. We can't afford to turn vast areas of our planet into unusable moonscape depositories of lethal nuclear waste materials.

Solar energy is abundant and pervasive, but its supply varies from day to night and season-to-season and is compromised by clouds over many of the most energy needy areas. With present technologies solar energy could supply only a fraction of the world demand. Already China's energy consumption and demand are growing rapidly. Even so, research into electrically linking sun-rich areas with those less well endowed should be high priority.

Interesting research and experimentation is underway to produce hydrogen directly from solar energy. The efficiency of this process still is too low and the costs too high to be practical in a world that is rapidly increasing its energy dependence. This important research obviously must go on, but we should not even think about it as a panacea for our energy crunch!

Toffler, in his The Third Wave, discusses innovative bio-gas technologies that are successfully bringing energy to people in India's dispersed villages. I saw the same when I was in India on a research project in 1979. European countries are developing bio-waste conversion into gas. Research also is intensive in converting bio-waste materials into gas and diesel fuel. Toffler acknowledges the depletion of petroleum reserves in the near-term future and predicts that biology will replace petroleum in production of many items for our daily living. (31) In the Midwestern "Corn belt" of the United States the potential of

ethanol, made from corn, is touted as offering a significant boost to the country's energy needs. However, research suggests that at present it takes more
energy to produce a gallon of ethanol than is gained by the process.

Biology may be able to help, but the biomass alternative can not supply the
prodigious and increasing energy needs of the human family. After all, we
must leave most of the Earth in rainforests and other green vegetation to continue the conversion of carbon dioxide to oxygen, which humans also need!
Bio-based plastics increasingly are replacing metals in machinery, automobiles, utensils, and many common items, thereby reducing the pressure for new
metal production. However, there also are limits to bio-mass production for
energy and manufacturing inasmuch as foods all living creatures need are biol-
ogy-based!

Volcanic eruptions are evidence that exceedingly high temperatures persist in
the Earth's magma only a few thousand feet below the Earth's surface. The
potential for harnessing that energy source presents a challenge. With research
on the Earth's interior and possible development of new technologies, future
generations might be able to supply most of their energy needs by tapping into
this seemingly unlimited source.

Clearly a major energy breakthrough in any energy source would be far more
important to the human family's future than the development of more
deadly military devices or futile, wasteful research for a shield against incom-
ing rockets!

However, our energy related problems do not end with developing energy
alternatives to the fossil fuels. Fossil fuel emissions have increased seven-fold
since World War II and are changing the composition of the atmosphere. It is
these emissions that are causing Global Warming. There were thoughtful people in times past who insisted that the Earth was flat! And there are some "scientists" even now who disbelieve the impressive evidence about global
warming.

We have emphasized several times in this book that all facets of our natural
and cultural environments are interwoven with all others. In our use of the
Earth's resources we humans have been like babes in the woods. We have
unthinkingly destroyed the productivity of many parts of the Earth and
"moved on" to virgin territory, an option no longer available. We have used
resources and increased our numbers with no thought of tomorrow. We must
start thinking about the tomorrows yet to come and the kind of life we hope
our children and grand children will want to enjoy.

Too many folks, looking to the past and the future, have the notion that new scientific discoveries and inventions will come along just in time to solve our problems with food and water supply, with environmental degradation, with global warming, and with energy and other resources in short supply. That is a hope of fools. We should never pin our future on "maybes" or on a "technological possibility" or a "potential break-through" or "research underway". The future we leave for our children is at stake.

Even as we adopt ways to control the growth of population, use the Earth in sustainable ways, crank up research on alternative energy needs, and deal seriously with global warming, we should make plans for the future based only on technologies already in place or that we have ready and can put in place. We should stop wasting our treasure on military ventures that do not solve problems. We must use our treasure on people needs and leave our security to a Limited World Government!

The human record of dealing with our Earth and each other has known too much waste, greed, stupidity and killing. Because our numbers were small for thousands of years, our greed, waste, ignorance and wars made little difference to natural processes on our planet. That is not the case now. Our children and grandchildren must depend on the same Earth on which we depend and they *must* get along with others on this planet. It behooves us therefore to take care of the Earth—and ourselves—and present the Earth and the positives in our cultural accumulation to our children in as good condition as possible.

Robert F. Kennedy said this about our environmental challenge:

> "If we want to provide our children with the same opportunities for dignity and enrichment as those our parents gave us, we've got to start protecting the air, water, wildlife, and landscapes that connect us to our natural values and character. It's that simple." (32)

3. OUR HUMAN FAMILY. We humans are here as the result of a long evolutionary saga in a very unique environment from the simplest of life forms to ourselves. We can even view the human saga on Earth as an experiment that is still underway with the results still unknown as to whether we will be successful or not in developing a global civilization with peace and caring among all people that can go on successfully for thousands of years.

FRAGILE CARGO

Our human family...
    Five hundred generations
    Of genetic evolution
    And genetic roulette,
A genetic glitch here,
    A mutation there,
    And here we are!

A fragile, vulnerable cargo of life
    Sharing a common destiny
    With all living things
    On our jewel in space,
Diverse in color, stature, talent,
    Some with short lives, others longer,
    Some live weak, others stronger;

All depending desperately
    On an Earthly niche and
    On Earth's renewing bounty,
An Earth that to the human clan
    Knows no special mercy
    For wastage, greed, or stupidity.

David E. Christensen
May 9, 1994

My poem is one perspective on the long train of human experience on Earth. It is the purpose of these next pages to emphasize aspects of the world's human population that make it difficult to balance the equation between the needs of all living things—including ourselves—and the Earth's capacity to fulfill our needs, repair itself and retain its productivity.

The human family is obviously in its infancy in coming to grips with that equation. For too long there was land elsewhere for the taking—sometimes by force—and little heed was given to control population growth.

But that equation is critical for our future. We must control our numbers so that we may develop a plan to use our Earth home to sustain us indefinitely into the future. That must be the goal. Failing to fulfill that goal will leave only tragedy for our children and those who follow.

Norman Cousins saw the problem of sovereign nations trying to deal with this equation and how people deal with their Earth home. He came down on the side of world government as an answer.

> "Humanity needs world order. The fully sovereign nation is incapable of dealing with the poisoning (or depletion) of the earth….The management of the planet….requires a world government." (33)

Old Testament prophets railed against the kings and priests of their time who were mistreating the poorest of their subjects. The prophets told kings and priests what would happen if they did not make changes. At the beginning of PART II, "The Earth Versus People", several individuals were listed and identified as "prophets" admonishing us to take care of our Earth home—or else! Many modern day columnists and writers also are prophets calling attention to unwise government policies relating to the inequities of our social systems to those in need.

Among these modern day social critics and prophets I would list the following, in no particular order: Mahatma Gandhi, Morris Dees, Aung San Suu Kyi, Jim Hightower, Molly Ivins, Arundhati Roy, Benjamin Franklin (not the original one), Helen Thomas, Martin Luther King, Paul Krugman, and Michael Moore. And my apology to other modern day "prophets" whom I have not named.

Paul Simon had this to say about the "human family":

> "We occasionally hear the phrase 'the human family', suggesting that all of us have a kinship, implying that we should work together and get to understand each other better. That sounds so obvious it is almost trite to repeat. But a family that lives under one roof ultimately cannot be healthy in physical goods or mental attitude if it does not recognize its involvement in the larger family. St. Paul talks about 'the whole family in heaven and earth'". (34)

We can enlarge Paul Simon's "all of us living under one roof" concept to: "we all live under the same sky". We humans are one large and diverse "family" living under the Earth's one sky. As members of the same family, we depend very much on each other.

Each member of this large human family deserves to be treated with justice and to have an opportunity to develop his or her unique talents to the full. And no one should have to endure discrimination or a limitation of opportunities because of gender, race, religion, ethnicity, or sexual orientation. Only by respecting each other and using our many talents will we be able to reconcile differences among ourselves and with our Earth and move on to develop a peaceful world.

No branch of the human family should feel that it is better than any of the others or that it has all the answers. There are older and younger members of the human family "at the table". Humans come in all colors. We come from very large and very small nations. We can learn much from each other from the diversity of cultures gathered at today's table. We *must* learn from each other if we are to solve the problems we face together.

But entirely apart from our diversity, our diverse talents and everyone's need for food, water, shelter and hope is the problem that there are so many of us and our numbers are increasing so rapidly. Everyone should be familiar with the graph of world population growth since ancient times. [Figure 1] The effect of the earliest humans on the natural environment was similar to that of other animals. The human population was kept in check by accidents, diseases, plagues, attacks by other animals, tribal wars and starvation. Population increases were very gradual until the advent of the Industrial Revolution in the 1800s and its bourgeoning use of fossil fuels. Since the middle of the nineteenth century, world population has grown sharply so that now the growth line on a population graph rises almost vertically.

In a few parts of the world (Japan, North America, Europe, Australia and a few others) population growth is slow or has stabilized. However, total world population growth is cause for alarm for our children and those who follow. When I was born in 1921 the world's population was less than 2 billion. In 1990 the world's population was 5.3 billion. In the year 2000 it was 6.1 billions and in 2003 is estimated to be 6.3 billions. That represents a *daily* net growth of about 220,000 individuals during the decade of the 1990s. It is projected that growth will be about 210,000 *per day* between 2000 and 2010, with most of the growth taking place in Latin America, Africa and Asia. Just think of it: A new city the size of Waco, Texas, or Ashville, North Carolina, or Springfield, Illinois, every day! That means that *every day* world production of food and energy and all other things must be increased to fulfill the *daily and life long* needs of over two hundred thousand new people!

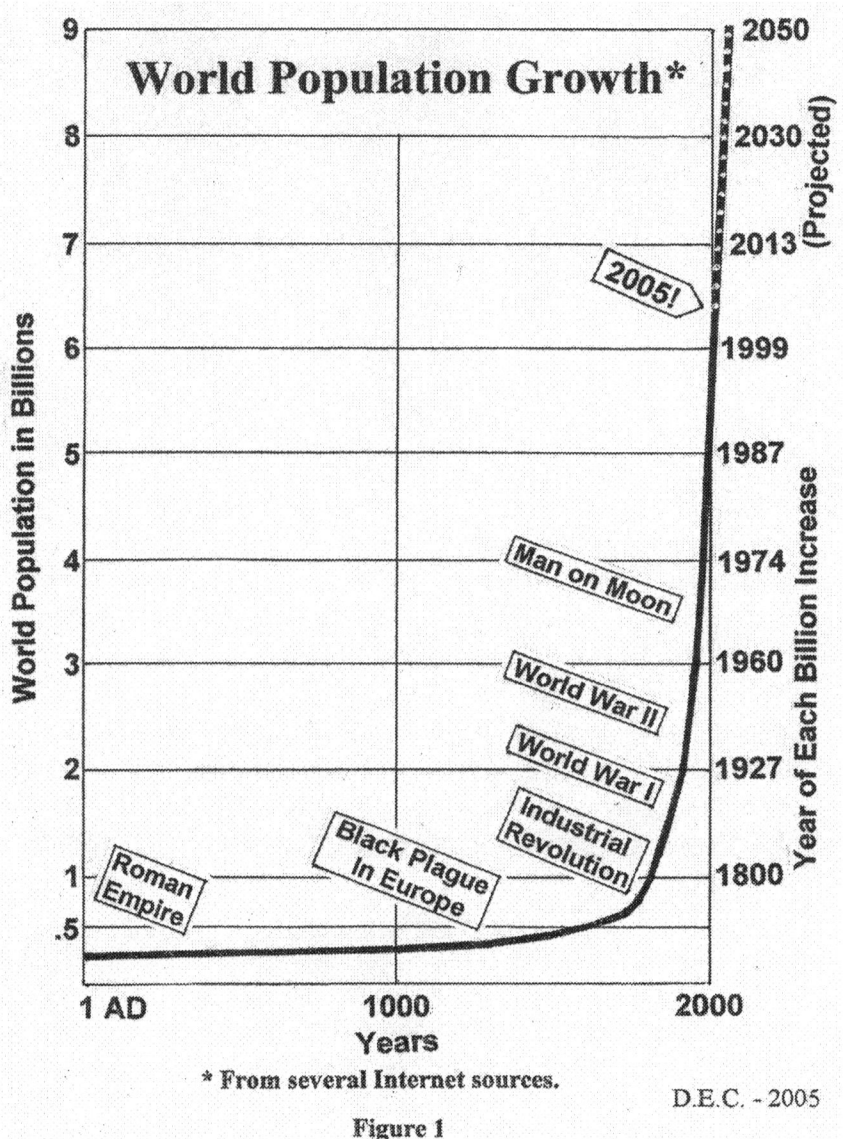

* From several Internet sources.

D.E.C. - 2005

Figure 1

And it is not just population totals that will cause problems for the future. Population in countries like the United States is divided into relatively equal age "cohorts"; that is, the numbers of children, young adults, older adults, and elderly are relatively even. In Japan and several European countries the average age of all persons is 39, with smaller numbers of children and young people. In a country like India, in contrast, children and youth far outnumber adults and the elderly. In fact, in several countries in Africa the average age of the total population is 15 or 16! This means there are far fewer adults to raise children and fewer adults to pay taxes to support schools, clinics, other community improvements and government services. It also indicates that much larger families are needed for their type of agriculture which is heavily dependant on hand labor. And as the children become parents, population gain rates are likely to be no less than they are today.

However, a tragic fact relates to that last statement. Especially in Sub-Saharan Africa, with AIDS and HIV having become such a devastating problem, the death of so many parents and bread winners actually puts many villages and communities "out of business". Communities—already with large numbers of children—are left mostly with children and grand parents and an inadequate basis for providing education, health care, or continuing sufficient economic activities of any kind. This is tragedy on the march, but the world has no way to deal with such a monumental scale of need. The UN is helping, but a Limited World Government might be able to do more.

There is an inverse correlation between education and income on the one hand and birth rate on the other. Countries (and individuals) with higher education levels also have higher income levels and lower birth rates than do countries (and individuals) with less education and income. Closely related to this correlation in TLA areas is the need to educate girls and women in matters of hygiene, business and birth control.

We must keep world population from outgrowing even further the Earth's resource base and the Earth's ability to repair itself. Ideally, people should be encouraged to have smaller families in an effort to reduce world population. This, of course, flies in the face of the need for many hands to sustain farm families in TLA areas. The answer appears to be simple: provide or improve education! On the one hand, reducing birth rates through birth control depends on education, and on the other hand, education opens individuals to new economic opportunities, thereby raising the levels of living. That is what happened in Europe and other "Westernized" countries during the last two centuries, and it is happening in other places today. However, to have access to an education will require significant changes in many countries. These must include changes in "attitudes" about women, about cultures with deep-seated male-dominance, about religious beliefs that hold people back from considering needed changes including birth control, about releasing TLA areas from control of the World Bank and IMF, and also about acceptance of change itself!

We must slow the growth of our human family so our generation might leave a better world for our children and those who will follow.

PART III

PROBLEMS MADE BY HUMANS MUST BE SOLVED BY HUMANS

To tackle these interlocked problems we should keep in mind Albert Einstein's sage advice: "We can't solve problems by using the same kind of thinking we used when we created them." (Internet) We also hear that it is a form of insanity to try to solve a problem using the same methods over and over that have not worked in the past (war, voluntary environmental controls, abstinence. etc.).

Part I dealt with the alarming way in which our Earth home is degenerating into extremes of the rich and the poor. Part II dealt with what this writer believes are the three greatest problems and challenges facing our country and the world in these beginning years of the twenty-first century. Few would question the urgency of our dealing with the war and terrorism issue, the corporate globalization juggernaut, or our environmental degradation and energy needs as they relate to the world's rapidly growing population.

Every one of these issues is fraught with challenges related directly to the short and long term security of the human family on this planet. These three issues can be dealt with only on a global basis, and that means some kind of world government, either an overhaul of the United Nations or establishing a new Limited World Government.

The challenge presented by these three issues is of such urgency that left unattended or dealt with in piecemeal fashion, any semblance of an orderly world will be lost in only a few decades. Normal "ways of life" will be deeply disrupted in both TA and TLA countries.

Supreme Court Justice William O. Douglas instructed us in 1952 that

> "Ideas are very dangerous; ideas have no boundaries—no state lines, no national lines, no oceans. They're powerful—the most powerful things in the world today. A few simple, good, old-fashioned ideas from the Declaration of Independence coupled with a fair portion of Point Four can stem the political tide of Communism (*or terrorism*). Take all the American money you can collect and all the guns and all the atomic bombs and keep your program sterile of these ideas of freedom and justice and opportunity—and the Red tide of Communism (*or terrorism*) will roll on and on and on. And that's what it's doing today. You can't stop it by talking about democracy and peace. You have to talk about it in terms that are understandable at the village level." (1) (Words in *italics* are mine. D.E.C.)

Note particularly William Douglas' assertion that Communism, the enemy of the time, will continue to roll on despite our arsenal of guns and bombs if we do not help the common people of the world at the village level with freedom, justice and opportunity. An arms race and threats is not the way to the hearts of people. You can add the Douglas quote to the three in "Our World of Extremes" relating to the "Revolution of Rising Expectations".

"Point Four", also mentioned by William Douglas, was the fourth "point" presented in President Truman's inaugural address on January 20, 1949. The first three "points" pledged: support for the UN, to continue world economic recovery, and to strengthen freedom-loving nations against aggression. "Point Four" proposed a bold new program of improve underdeveloped areas, an anti-dote to Communism (now terrorism) and the moral thing to do.

We may have been able to outspend the Soviet Union into bankruptcy through the arms race. But the terrorist threat presents a completely different kind of challenge. Our massive armaments are not the answer. An enormously expensive "missile shield" (still "being developed" and with several "it didn't work" tests) is not the answer against highly portable, inexpensive and lethal backpack or brief-case sized explosives. Our bluster and arrogance are not the answer. Preemptive invasions of small nations that have not harmed us directly are not the answer. Only by living up to our ideals and sharing more of our wealth do we have a chance against the dispersed terrorist arsenal of surprise attacks and fear.

We all should agree that the first step to solve any problem is to recognize and acknowledge that there is a problem that needs "fixing". War is such a problem and it has been acknowledged as a problem plaguing the human family from early times. In our time it can be solved! As Victor Hugo said, "An invasion of armies can be resisted, but not an idea whose time has come."

The problem of war and the other major problems are getting out of hand and must be solved soon, and no supernatural power is going to solve them for us. These problems are of our own making, and only wise decisions and actions and no doubt some compromises by humans—acting together around the globe—will get us out. Given the evidence, the time for a Limited World Government is not a "pie-in-the-sky" dream for "some time in the future". It is not a naïve idea of idealists. It is needed now!

Look back at the quotations from former generals, presidents and other world leaders near the beginning of "Part II, Three Key Problems". These eminent persons speak about the wastefulness of war, the tragedy of war, the foolishness of war, the uncontrollability of war, all of which go against everything civilization stands for. And because it commands so much of our attention and money, the war problem may be seen as the number one problem standing in the way of our solving other problems that plague the human family and our Earth home itself.

But how can we move toward realization of a Limited World Government?

A. STRUGGLES TOWARD WORLD PEACE

I was disappointed that in his book, <u>Earth in the Balance,</u> Former Senator and Vice President Al Gore in a few paragraphs pushed aside world government as a possible solution for the world's ecological crisis. He then posed this question, "What conceivable system of world governance would be able to compel individual nations to adopt environmentally sound policies?" (2) His answer was a strong statement against world government simply because he didn't see how it could work. Should the human family just give up, as Al Gore seems ready to, and let looming problems overwhelm us?

Speaking particularly about the environment, my response is that our global environmental problems can be dealt with *only* by nations working together within the structure of a Limited World Government. My further comment is that our "Earth versus the People" issues are so serious now that, if the human experiment on Earth is to have any hope of success, we MUST overcome obstacles to bring on a sustainable balance soon. And finally, I believe people (and their nations) can be educated to abide by world environmental standards as they come to understand it is vital that they do so.

The world's key environmental issues, like global warming and the limitations on supplies of fresh water and petroleum, can be dealt with only on a global basis and must be presented "to the people" honestly and clearly. Health and disease control can only be dealt with on a global basis. Multinational corporations can be turned to serve the common good only by a strong global institution.

Bringing Limited World Government to reality will be difficult and involve sacrifices by many. Limited World Government will gain in stature as it becomes evident it can eliminate war and make possible the solution of other important global issues.

Nations now take hard positions to protect their "sovereignty". However, with the deepening interdependence among nations and despite the sound and fury of politicians, the distorted concept of national sovereignty should not be invoked to interfere with what must be done by the people. Nations are made up of people, and when problems become critical enough—as they are now—the people and enlightened statesmen and women will take action toward a solution.

Several times in this book I have said that now is the time for a Limited World Government. Another quote comes to mind about how new ideas come to be accepted. Andrew Schopenhauer told us that

> "All truth passes through three states: First, it is ridiculed. Second, it is violently opposed. And third, it is accepted as self-evident." (3)

Two generations ago many people were aware of the world government issue. It was a hot issue. Then the Cold War grabbed our attention and our tax dollars for forty years from the early 1950s to 1990, when the Soviet Union imploded. During the decades of the Cold War two of the problems that sparked world government interest after World War II have become even more urgent (war and militarization and the human population versus Earth equation), and a new critical issue, corporation-dominated globalization, has reared its hydra-head.

With so many people having supported the world government idea in the past and with the same issues still "on the table", Limited World Government is no longer being ridiculed. It is in the second stage: Its truth is being weighed and opposed. Let us hope that in the not too distant future world government will move to Schopenhauer's third state of acceptance as self-evident!

1. GENERAL PEACE PLANS AND EFFORTS. Many large and small books have been written through the years presenting different views of the war problem and how to deal with it. For example, Lionel Curtis" omnibus, <u>World Order</u>, published in 1939, is three books in one. Curtis' three books present a detailed and orderly analysis of the history of the world from prehistoric beginnings of village government to the world of the 1930s. Tracing the evolution of ever-larger political units, he concludes with a strong endorsement of a global commonwealth based on the model of the British Commonwealth of Nations and the United States. He suggests such a commonwealth could emerge with only a few English-speaking nations joining together. However, Curtis is not hopeful common people even in enlightened nations can or will act in their own interest to move their governments toward establishment of

such a global commonwealth. He sees religion as the vehicle through which a caring and cooperative spirit among people must be generated toward the establishment of such a global commonwealth. (4)

<u>Searchlight on Peace Plans: Choose Your Road to World Government</u> was printed in 1949 during the post-World War II flurry of interest in world government. Written by Edith Wynner and Georgia Lloyd, this book is a compilation of "peace plans" that have been put forward since earliest times, but especially since 1914. (5) The authors demonstrate that the idea of eliminating war has been on the human agenda for a long time, and with each effort we may be getting closer to eliminating war and organizing for world peace.

Harlan Cleveland's 1976 book, <u>The Third Try at World Order</u>, accepts the League of Nations and the United Nations as the world's first two "tries" toward a world order. Because of significant changes that took place between the end of World War II and 1976 (the despoilment of nature, our awareness of nature's limitations, and what Cleveland calls the "fairness revolution", the equivalent to the "Revolution of Rising Expectations" among the world's less well-off people), his book presents a plan for a "third try" at world order. (6) However, even acknowledging the increasing interdependence among people and nations and a review of critical issues, he ends his study with a call for existing national governments to work harder at resolving issues, with no mention of world government.

Garry Davis' second book, <u>World Government Ready or Not!</u>, published in 1984, does look critically at world problems and acknowledges world government as the only logical solution. However, Davis' book is not a "how to" book with analyses, strategies, priorities and steps for achieving a world government. His book is an insightful collection of pieces about Garry Davis' decades of work to inform and raise consciousness about world government and what it might offer if it is achieved. Davis' "World Service Authority", operating out of an office in Washington, D.C., has provided thousands of "World Passports", "World Citizen Cards", "World Birth Certificates", "World ID Cards", and other documents that have helped those desiring official world-embracing IDs. (7)

A small paperback also needs mention. In 1986 Thomas A. Hudgens published a revised edition of <u>Let's. Abolish. War: We Need L.A.W.</u>, with L.A.W. having a double meaning: representing the word "law" and also the words "Let's Abolish War". Hudgens book develops the need to abolish war simply because of the human and other wastage war causes. He includes many quotes that support the need to abolish war and the need for laws that apply to the whole world. He notes a 1983 poll that showed 67% of Americans favored strengthening the UN so it could do the job for which it was established. (Recent polls have shown the same level of support.) His book concludes with a primary suggestion to push legislators to support reforming the UN into a federal world government so it *can* do its job. (8)

2. THE CHALLENGE BEFORE OUR THIRTEEN COLONIES AND NOW. As was mentioned, in 1781, at the close of the Revolutionary War, representatives of the thirteen colonies passed the Articles of Confederation and the new nation was born. After a few years our Founding Fathers saw the confederacy not working well. At a Constitutional Convention in Philadelphia in 1787 a new constitution establishing and empowering a central government was agreed upon. The new Constitution came into effect on June 21, 1788 when it had been ratified by nine of the thirteen original states. It has been amended twenty seven times, and here we are today.

The need now, even more than was the case after World Wars I and II, is for the world's people to understand and acknowledge that a new level of law and government—above the nations—is desperately needed if we are ever to tame the war god Mars, rein in Globalization so it will serve all the people, and deal in time with our energy crisis and the serious ecological problems we have caused to our Earth home.

We humans, working together, need to do this soon before "Western Civilization" reaches a crisis point. Crisis points could come from any of the following: 1. An energy shortage and the depletion of cheap oil, 2. A pull-back or pullout of huge foreign investments that have helped the U.S. finance (and gloss over) its massive national debt, 3. By the growing worldwide insufficiency of fresh water, 4. By an outbreak of another life-threatening disease around the world, or 5. By massive disruptions from cumulative effects of global warming. The key point of this book is that the world's people are likely to face more than one of these in the next decade or two.

These are critical and challenging times and we should be using our ingenuity to resolve these critical issues rather than feeding an endless military appetite that really accomplishes nothing positive. We should be turning from "making swords" to seeking desperately needed global solutions to problems that are with us today and could overwhelm the world and undo a potential good life for everyone on the planet.

3. EVOLUTION OF INTERNATIONAL COOPERATION. The first serious but very piece-meal efforts at organizing agencies through which nations

could cooperate on particular topics of mutual concern began in the latter decades of the nineteenth century. In 1864 following the 1854–56 Crimean War and near the end of the American Civil War, Florence Nightingale organized the International Red Cross. This was followed quickly by the International Telecommunications Union in 1865, and in 1875 and 1878 by the International Postal Union, the International Bureau of Weights and Measures and the International Meteorological Organization. In 1919 the International Civil Aviation Organization and International Labor Organization were formed.

These need to be mentioned individually to demonstrate the manner in which new technologies in communications and travel among nations naturally brought along the need to deal, not only with humanitarian issues on which the Red Cross focused, but also with international mail delivery, standardization of weights and measures to facilitate trade, weather reporting, civil aviation and labor issues. The more the people of the world exchange goods and travel, the more social machinery needs to be invented to help things run smoothly between and among nations. All of these agencies are indicators of the increasing interdependence among nations that has taken place in the last century and a half.

The League of Nations was formed in 1920 in the hope of eliminating war from the Earth. However, despite the United States having been one of the strongest proponents of such an organization, the U.S. did not join. The League also had other problems and structural flaws, principally that it was a confederation of nations, and members supported it or not at their convenience.

4. THE UNITED NATIONS (UN): SUCCESSES AND WEAKNESSES. With great anticipation and world wide enthusiasm the United Nations was formed in 1945 at the close of World War II. Since its inception, and although most Americans have continued to support it, the UN has always been under attack by its opponents. Norman Cousins summarized the UN's predicament when he wrote:

> "If the United Nations is to survive, those who represent it must bolster it; those who advocate it must submit to it; and those who believe in it must fight for it." (9)

Like its predecessor the League of Nations, the UN is only a confederation of member nations. It has no power to enforce its actions except as member nations (especially the five veto-holding members) agree to provide that support. A quote from one of President Eisenhower's books is instructive, although we must be reminded that General Eisenhower commanded the forces of only three English-speaking nations in preparing for and carrying out the "D Day" Normandy invasion in June 1944.

> "During the war it was demonstrated that international unity of purpose and execution could be attained, without jeopardy to any nation's independence, if all were willing to pool a portion of their authority (sovereignty!) in a single headquarters with power to enforce their decisions. In the formation of the new United Nations and of the Allied organization for the control of Germany, this lesson has not yet been accepted. Its application would have meant some form of limited federated world government, which, while conforming to the Western Allies battle front experience as providing the only sure way to success, was politically unacceptable to any of the great nations concerned." (10) (Underlining by D.E.C.)

Based on their GDP, member nations are levied annual dues for the UN's operations and additional amounts for peacekeeping and other programs to which the UN is committed. However, if any UN member nation does not like a particular policy of the UN or one of its agencies, it can simply decide not to pay its share of that budget. During the Reagan presidency the U.S. withdrew from UNESCO because of the UN's support of abortion as a part of the UN's family planning program. The U.S. for years has criticized the administration of the UN and withheld at least part of our nation's dues for general UN operations and peacekeeping, thus weakening the UN's effectiveness and opening it to further criticism. According to a Global Policy Reform report (on the Internet), as of March 31, 2005, United States arrears, totaling over $1.5 billions, represented 51% of all member arrears to the UN.

By what has been described it is clear the UN is beholden to its most powerful, veto holding members—especially the United States. The UN has no direct source of revenue for its operations, and any one of the five permanent members of the Security Council can stop any UN action they oppose.

These are serious flaws when one reflects that the UN was formed to eliminate war between major powers. Since its beginnings in 1945 the UN has been successful in negotiating cease-fires and peace agreements in dozens of conflicts around the world that involve small nations. And in the half-century since its formation, the UN's numerous agencies have helped millions of people in many ways. However, its members did not permit it to act against the genocide in Rwanda and is stymied again in Sudan's Darfur. And, as was evident in

President G.W.Bush's starting a preemptive war against Iraq in February 2003, the UN is not able to stop a "big power" from doing whatever it is determined to do.

B. FERMENT TOWARD "PEACE ON EARTH"

The deaths and devastation of World War I brought on the formation of the League of Nations. The devastation, deaths and the awesome power of the atom bomb that ended World War II inspired the formation of the United Nations and also brought on an active movement toward world government in England and the United States.

The late 1940s were "heady" times in South Chicago and many other places in the United States and the United Kingdom. Those were days when Carol, my wife, and I first learned about world government at tent meetings on the Mall by the University of Chicago where I was a graduate student in Geography. We became active in the fledgling "World Republic" organization, in 1946 or 1947.

The ferment for world government seemed to be everywhere. Articles appeared in many magazines, books were written on the subject, including Emery Reves' Anatomy of Peace, which went through eight printings in 1945 and 1946. Reves' book was lauded by Senators, clergy and professors; a condensed version was carried in three consecutive issues of the Readers Digest beginning in December 1945; a special large print "king size" version was published in 1946; and for weeks Reves' book was on top of the New York Times and New York Herald best seller lists.

Reves' book starts with different interpretations of the years between World Wars I and II. Each account is from the viewpoint of a particular country, the United States, Great Britain, France, Germany and the Soviet Union. Each interpretation justifies everything that nation did and finds fault with others for bringing on World War II.

Reves summarizes his analysis as follows:

> "A careful study of human history reveals that the assumption that war is inherent in human nature—and therefore eternal—is shallow and faulty, that it is only a superficial impression....
>
> "The real cause of all wars has always been the same. They have occurred with the regularity of a natural law at clearly determined moments as the result of clearly definable conditions....
>
> "1. Wars between groups of men forming social units always take place when these units-tribes, dynasties, churches, cities, nations—exercise unrestricted sovereign power.
>
> "2. Wars between these social units cease the moment sovereign power is transferred from them to a larger or higher unit." (11)

During the "heady" late 1940s and early 1950s there were many university and local round-table discussion groups, seminars, and meetings at which the pros and cons of world government were discussed as well as the causes of war and the inadequacies of the UN. There was a feeling that, whereas World War I had failed to be "the war to end all war", we must do better following World War II. There was optimism that it could be done and that a Limited World Government offered a realistic answer. As was mentioned, in November 1948 the people of Connecticut voted 12 to 1 in favor of strengthening the UN to prevent war. A news item at that time reported:

> "On the day after election, the commentators were too busy explaining that Harry Truman was still President to pay any attention to an interesting political development in the state of Connecticut. Along with the newspapers, they ignored what turned out to be the only real landslide victory in the nation. The victor in this one-sided election contest was, oddly enough, not a candidate for public office. It was a referendum proposal to change the United Nations into a limited World Government, and it won by a vote of 130,548 to 11,467—an almost 12-to-1 margin." (12)

Connecticut's remarkable news was overshadowed by President Harry Truman's surprise victory over New York Governor Thomas Dewey.

Reves analyzes "sovereignty" and notes that with the passing of the divine right of kings, it is the PEOPLE who hold sovereignty in a democracy. The co-opting of sovereignty from the people to a nation's government and government institutions is an aberration that needs correction in the people's understanding. Let me repeat this very important principle: In a democracy it is the PEOPLE who are sovereign, not their government or its institutions. Read again our Declaration of Independence!

Thus, if the "people" are willing to transfer some of their "sovereignty" to a higher government, they may do so. Keep that in mind as I discuss different ways in which a Limited World Government might be brought into being.

Ronald Glossop reports that between 1941 and 1950 TWENTY TWO American state legislatures passed resolutions urging United States participation in a world federation. He also notes that the United States House of Representatives held hearings in 1948 and 1949 and supported U.S. participation in a world federation, and that the Senate held hearings in 1950. (13) But all of this came to an end with the Korean conflict and the furor and hype that came on with Senator Joseph McCarthy's Communist "witch hunts". "Communism" became the new enemy. Interest in world government was set aside by fear and militarization.

1. INTERNATIONAL LAW. Mahatma Gandhi and Martin Luther King introduced to the world a vision of non-violence as a means to gain needed humane reforms for the people from unresponsive governments. Their visions were finally successful. After years of confrontations with British forces, colonial India gained its independence from Great Britain in 1947. And some basic civil rights were gained for blacks in the United States in the 1960s.

But could non-violent protests have been successful against Hitler, who gassed millions of non-violent German citizens, or Stalin, who executed thousands of Soviet citizens? Is there any way non-violent protests might have helped in Kosovo, Rwanda, or even now in Darfur or Iraq? In my judgment the answer to these questions is: Without strong pressure from the international community of nations—especially the more powerful nations—or from a recognized world body with power, it is unlikely that non-violent protests would have worked. There simply is no world agency with power to enforce International Law or declarations of Universal Human Rights.

International law has been slow to mature. In 1921 the "World Court" was established and began functioning in The Hague, Netherlands. This court's function was to adjudicate issues only between nations, but it had no means to enforce its judgments. Its functions were taken over in 1945 with the establishment of the UN and the "International Court of Justice" (ICJ), which also operates out of The Hague. However, like the former "World Court", the ICJ deals only with issues between nations and has no power to enforce its judgments.

The Geneva Convention, agreed to in 1929 by many nations, sets forth standards to deal with prisoners of war. This convention has been viewed as a necessary piece of a developing code of international law, but there is no world legal structure to enforce its dozens of articles. In recent years the United States has openly thumbed its nose on Geneva Convention standards (Guantanamo, etc.). This seems foolish because our government expects others to treat United States prisoners of war by Geneva Convention standards.

UN resolutions and sanctions were passed against Saddam Hussein's regime for actions against the Kurds and Kuwait, but Saddam ignored them. In the 1980s President Reagan's administration ignored UN resolutions calling for a cessation of our covert war (through the "contra") against Nicaragua's government. President Reagan also ignored a World Court decision that condemned the United States' 1984 bombing of Nicaragua's Corinto harbor.

The UN Security Council (usually with the United States abstaining) has passed several resolutions over the years criticizing Israel and the Palestinians regarding their hostile actions against the other. UN resolutions also have repeatedly called on Israel to halt construction of Jewish settlements on Palestinian lands, but Israel continues to establish new settlements. And in July 2004 the International Court of Justice directed Israel to tear down the massive wall Israel was constructing on Palestine land to protect its (illegal) Jewish settlements. Israel ignores these judgments and construction of the "Berlin-like wall" continues.

In July 2002 the International Criminal Court (ICC) entered into force. President Clinton signed the Rome Statute of the International Criminal Court (ICC) on behalf of the American people as he was leaving office in 2000. Although the United States had been prominent in the establishment of this court, President G. W. Bush withdrew United States support, perhaps fearful that he or other Americans might be charged with war crimes. Apparently President Bush chose to ignore the court's proviso that the International Criminal Court would take on a case *only* if the government of the individual charged did not take up the case. The International Court of Justice seems to be functioning well without the United States, but it too has no means to enforce its judgments.

The years since World War II also have been fruitful in bringing forth, on a range of topics, a cluster of treaties that add to the flimsy but growing fabric of "international law". The United States signed the following but these have not been ratified by the Senate: 1977—International Covenant on Economic,

Social and Cultural Rights in (CESCR); 1980—Convention on Discrimination Against Women (CEDAW); 1995—Convention on Rights of the Child; 1996—Comprehensive Test Ban Treaty; and 1998—Kyoto Protocol (to control global warming and the "Greenhouse Effect"). Perhaps the Senate is sensitive to the mythical issue of "sovereignty".

The United States remains one of a very few nations that has not signed or ratified the ICC or the Land Mine Ban Treaty. By not signing these treaties we remain in the company of such nations as China, Cuba, North Korea, Pakistan and Russia. We have signed only the UN Framework Convention on Climate Control (1992) and the Chemical Weapons Convention (1997). In the several efforts listed toward establishing international law on critical issues it is clear that the United States is the only major power lagging behind.

Since there is no global institution with power to enforce court judgments or UN resolutions, or to act on behalf of a people being slaughtered by genocide, true "international law" remains only a hope. That hope can be fulfilled by a Limited World Government. Humanity is at another crux point in history. Establishing global law is our only viable option for a peaceful world for our children and those who follow.

2. THE POWER OF RELIGION. Henry Wallace told us:

> "Religion is a great force (for good) even though evil or misguided men have used that force against humanity from time to time.
> "I believe that the doctrine of the brotherhood of man justifies the concept of ultimate world citizenship and that the various workers of the world will eventually look on themselves as a unit regardless of nationality." (14)

By its very nature and its importance in the lives of most people, organized religion *can* offer a path of possible reconciliation as the world's people, with their diverse cultures, together seek more peaceful lives.

The December 2004 tsunami that struck South Asia so devastatingly caused many people to raise religious questions. Why would a loving God let this happen? Why did it overwhelm this village and spare that one? We must assume that if there is one God, it is the same God for all living things and all religions and for all time. Such a God can not play favorites. In my view, and with due respect to others who may have a different view, "God" and the universe are "neutral" in dealings with the human family. It is up to us to make things work here on Earth.

Humans simply are, at least for now, the "top dog" among creatures on this planet, and whether we remain so depends entirely on us. We, among all animals and living things, have the capacity to consider all kinds of questions, such as: Why are we here? What can we do to make our being here a success? But are enough of us even asking that second question?

Kurt Vonnegut, an American writer, asked his grown son, Mark, the first question and got this simple and direct reply: "We are here to help each other through this thing, whatever it is." (15) Nothing religious or mythological. Nothing about heaven or hell. No speculation. Mark's reply is simple, direct and positive, with spiritual subtleties. Even if one has no religious affiliation, such a belief can be the basis of a good and successful life.

An interesting aspect of three of the world's major religions is that they agree on some important precepts. Judaism, Christianity and Islam acknowledge common beginnings in the Old Testament story of Abraham. All three profess a version of the "Golden Rule" in human relations. And yet, their histories include times when they encouraged mayhem on "non-believers". The Crusades and the Inquisition were "religion-driven" by Catholic Christians in Europe. Russia's pogrom against the Jews early last century and Germany's Holocaust were government-driven programs to eliminate those of the Hebrew faith. Sub-groups within the three major religions have fought battles against other sub-groups of the same religion. Catholics and Protestants have a long history of battles and some, as in Ireland, smolder to this day. Among Muslims, Sunnis and Shiites do not get along well. And from Israel's inception in 1947 Hasidic and Reformed Jews have struggled together to try to make their small country work.

But where does religion fit into a "healing the world" theme? Religious institutions compete with each other for member and power. In their independence and "sovereignty" religious institutions are a bit like nations. However, the dozens if not hundreds of splits and splinters over the centuries give testimony to the reality that an individual's religion is a very personal matter.

Through the centuries some things have changed. Repelled by their European experience, the forefathers of the United States believed the "separation of church and state" concept would quell frictions between competing religious groups and prevent one from becoming dominant in their new country. Our first amendment guarantees the right of free speech and "freedom of religion". However, maintaining that principle has not been easy.

In times past it was common that religious and government leaders worked together and sometimes were the same person. And through the centuries businesses and religious institutions have tried to gain favors from their governments because of the power of government and its "deep pockets". Even in the face of a separation of church and state, it is happening now in the United States with funding for "faith based" services to provide help for those in need.

In 1893 the first "Parliament of World Religions" was held in Chicago in conjunction with the World's Fair. Representatives of all major religions were represented and others as well. However, no summary paper or publication came from that meeting.

More recently, in 1970, there was a meeting of adherents to many faiths, including Bahai, Buddhism, Islam, Hebrew, Confucian, Christian, Shintoist, and even Zoroastrian. The goal of the meeting was to distill the common beliefs from all religions. Those attending did agree on a set of seven beliefs or principles that are basic to all civilized, caring communities (Appendix B1).

In 1993 a meeting called "The Second Parliament of World Religions" was held in Chicago. This was an eight-day event. Seven thousand seven hundred participants representing about two hundred fifty different religious traditions were present. The purpose of the meeting was to distill from the world's religions the moral and ethical roots that could give direction to the lives of all humans now and into the future. They called their distillation "The Declaration of a Global Ethic", and they, too, came out with seven statements or "declarations" (Appendix B2).

A third Parliament of World Religions convened in Capetown, South Africa, in 1999 and another convened in Barcelona, Spain, in 2004. Key themes discussed in 1999 were: pursuit of world peace, improved environmental stewardship, global sustainability and fair economic practices. Key topics in 2004 were: religious violence, access to safe water, fate of refugees and the elimination of developing countries' debts. Notice that most of the topics discussed in both 1999 and 2004 were not about theology; they were about people and environmental issues.

The simple fact of their repeated meetings makes these Parliaments very important, and they must continue. Most members of the human family are affiliated with one of the world's major religious institutions. If all major religious institutions would teach their adherents about justice and the importance of understanding and accepting those of different faiths and the commonalities of their different messages, the world's cleavages might be narrowed.

Can we hope that some day the human family will come together and try to live by the overlapping fourteen points of the earlier Parliaments of World Religions? Can we hope that people of all faiths will work with their leaders to address the fairness and environmental issues that must be faced? Through our religions all of us could make these things happen, and we then could be on the threshold of having a truly caring global community, with war an activity in the past and a Limited World Government in place acting for all of the world's people.

Christianity and Islam hinge on stories from the life and teachings of Jesus and Mohammed, while Judaism evolved from the concept that the Hebrews were God's chosen people. One wonders what religious repercussions will ensue on Earth when we ultimately make contact with intelligent creatures on other planets, who surely will have developed their own religions.

In a May 2003 Wiley cartoon and amidst billowing clouds, a new arrival to heaven stands on the threshold and looks at a large sign. A heavenly welcomer, presumably representing the many religions of those in heaven, says to a newcomer, "Ironically, that's what makes it so peaceful here." And the sign says: "Welcome to heaven. Keep your religion to yourself."

There are many paths up the mountain of ethical living and helping others. One does not even need to be "religious" in a formal sense to be trudging up that mountain of fairness, justice and sharing. We should help others on their way while respecting the many differences in religious traditions and beliefs that are held by our neighbors and people around the world as they trudge up the same mountain.

3. THE NEED FOR LIMITED WORLD GOVERNMENT. The hope for "Peace on Earth" and justice for all can be fulfilled only when individuals, following their highest impulses, help their governments to help those in need and work toward global law, with justice for all.

Given the evidence, global law is not a notion of naïve idealists. It is not a "pie-in-the-sky" dream for "sometime in the future"!

As difficult as it will be to bring it on, establishing global law through a Limited World Government is a "must do" idea. It is our only viable option if our children and those who follow are to have a chance to live in peace.

C. EDUCATION, HEALTH CARE AND PEACE.

1. EDUCATION. Essential in today's world is the need for all people to gain a fair and unbiased understanding of other countries and cultures. Thus other issues, like the need for education and health care, also need serious simultaneous attention if we are to make progress on the three critical issues that have been cited.

With transportation and communication improvements of the last century and a half, we are told that—in effect—the world is getting smaller. I think it is the reverse. In earlier times knowledge was limited and much that was taught about the world and other people and cultures simply was prejudiced falsehood. I have some very old geography books as proof. International relations were limited and education was focused on one's country and region. Few people traveled so the misinformation had little international impact.

Now we must know the truth about countries and people everywhere on Earth. We must know about the condition of the Earth itself, and about new scientific discoveries that are affecting everyone's life in so many ways. Critical also is the need for birth control and health education that will help everyone to manage their future, but especially those in TLA countries.

Education must go far beyond simple literacy. Simple literacy education, with no underpinnings of fairness and a reasonable worldview, may have been adequate for our pioneer forebears. But learning only to read and write leaves a half-educated person vulnerable to propaganda, half-truths and the ranting of demagogic leaders. Madrases in the Middle East, where mostly boys from poorer families learn literacy and hate, are fertile ground for bringing on another generation of terrorists. Simple literacy and one-time job training are no longer adequate for the complex world of the 21st Century. Further, any form of education that teaches or implies superiority of one ethnic or religious or national group over another is not serving its students well for the future.

To remain healthy and survive, democracies must depend on the good judgment of an informed electorate. And to have an informed electorate a country and community must have good schools that will help children and young people gain knowledge and learn to think for themselves and be concerned about others.

Edward Higbee observed that "The average school can cope with illiteracy but it is neither staffed nor designed to develop able and imaginative minds, yet these are truly the hope of mankind." (16) We know that some leaders brag about their having been "C" students. And I know that some very bright people just let themselves "slide by" in school. However, the quality of our future, in the United States and the world, depends in large measure on whether our more gifted children and young people gain the knowledge and hone their intellects to be good leaders in the years ahead.

There is a pathetic monument on the campus of the Southern Illinois University in Carbondale. It is in memory of five foreign students who died in a dormitory fire in 1992. The message on the monument reads, "The world will never know what their young lives could have given." How true. That is so true for any young person who is unable to develop his or her talents to the full. The world has so many problems that call for all the bright, inquiring and innovative young people we can help develop!

2. HEALTH CARE. Just like air and water and birds that fly, diseases do not honor the political boundaries people have made all over the Earth. As with other problems cited, the only possibility for at least partial control of highly contagious diseases is to control movement of goods and people that might carry germs of one kind or another.

There also is the problem of "alien species" (creatures and plants being moved unwittingly by all means of transportation) crossing borders. Control of international movements of people and goods can best be managed through a Limited World Government. However, even with controls, the problem of "alien species" no doubt would continue.

Democracies especially depend on educated citizens who study issues and vote intelligently. However, whether or not an individual will take advantage of education that is offered and can get and hold a job (and pay taxes) will depend in part on his or her health. And one's health, in turn, will depend on nutrition during growing up years, on family income and the education of parents. In too many places one's health and health care still relate to one's race. All of these are part of the interconnected web of factors affecting health and education that have repercussions in international affairs.

The professions of medicine and health care have come a long way through the centuries and especially in recent decades. Research on new medical procedures and pharmaceuticals has brought remarkable results. Many today remember when dentists' use of pain killers was not too effective, if they were used at all. Many remember the early death sentence that heart problems or diabetes laid on an individual. And we remember sanitariums for tuberculosis, the stigma of mental illness and grim stories about "insane asylums".

In some TLA areas, shamans and witch doctors still are called upon to deal with human ailments. The progress that was made in TLA areas in recent decades in teaching health and birth control basics is being reversed in some areas by the AIDs epidemic. As was mentioned, especially in Sub-Saharan Africa this epidemic is destroying villages and village culture by eliminating many individuals in the most productive and parenting years of their lives. Women, especially young married women, are primary victims from their husbands.

Health care, like education, is an essential service and every person in the world should have access to basic health services as a "right". The United States is the richest nation in the world and we are one of the few without a universal health care system to serve all of its citizens. Elderly and disabled Americans have health care insurance from federal programs (Medicare and Medicaid). Those still working may pay for health insurance directly or through their employers, but fewer employers are offering it. Over 45 million Americans have no health care coverage at all.

In virtually all TA countries it is taken for granted that health services are part of a government's responsibility. National government sponsored programs (not in the United States) may include, in addition to basic health services, strong "preventive medicine" and health education programs, eye care, dental care, prenatal care for mothers and care for infants. All of these save money in the long run by averting later problems, and they lead to a healthier work force and healthier children—who are the next generation's work force and who will learn more effectively if they have adequate health care.

D. CHARACTERISTICS OF A VIABLE "LIMITED WORLD GOVERNMENT"

When the United States government was formed under the new Constitution in 1788, the thirteen original colonies transferred some powers to the new central government. These included the power to tax, to control interstate and foreign trade, to manage defense and foreign policy, to establish a postal service, and the power to enforce order. A new level and type of court system also had to be established. All other powers remained with the states.

A new world government must also have specified limited powers; all other powers would remain with individual nations. Nations that join must transfer enough of their power to the new world government to provide "social and international order". We do not need to reinvent the UN or the League of Nations!

Once initiatives are taken to form a Limited World Government, by whatever means, it will take several years of phased steps before the new world government will become reality and be running reasonably smoothly. It will be a few more years before it will have proved its effectiveness. Only then can nations reduce their military establishments. It is likely to take even more years for the world's people to feel comfortable with and even feel some allegiance to the new global institution!

To fulfill its reason for being a Limited World Government must have powers (not granted to the UN) which replicate the three "balanced" elements of the United States government: A "Global Parliament" with definite powers, a chief executive and executive council, a court system to oversee implementation of global law (the ICJ and ICC are already in place). To fund its operations the new Limited World Government must have its own direct source of revenue to support its operations and its new a volunteer "Global Peace Force". Two other elements must be advanced along with these five for the success of the new world government. A phased general disarmament must follow soon after the establishment of a new world government. And a continuing commitment must be made by the new Limited World Government to <u>assist TLA areas toward improvements in their way of life</u>. These seven items are discussed briefly in the following pages.

1. GLOBAL PARLIAMENT. Guided by a Constitution, a Limited World Government will need a "Global Parliament" to deliberate and make decisions on behalf of the people of member nations and the world. For its decisions to be accepted as forming international law, the Global Parliament's voting procedure must meld three factors: population, economic power and nationhood, as proposed by Hudson and Schwartzberg in <u>Appendix C</u>.

2. CHIEF EXECUTIVE AND EXECUTIVE COUNCIL. The Limited World Government must have a Chief Executive, a staff, and an Executive Council. These could be patterned after the Secretariat and Security Council of the UN. The Executive Council would be empowered by the General Assembly to act on certain matters when the General Assembly is not in formal session and/or when a quick response to a world situation was called for. And the Chief Executive would serve as chief officer of the Limited World Government and, with the Executive Council, would approve or disapprove proposals of the Global Parliament. The Chief Executive's staff would maintain records and account books of the world government's activities and would have the responsibility to carry out peace keeping and other directives of the Global Parliament and the Executive Council through its various agencies and commissions.

3. GLOBAL COURT SYSTEM. The Limited World Government must have a court system in place to interpret and implement global law as that law relates to nations and individuals. The International Court of Justice (ICJ) and the new International Criminal Court (ICC) are in place and would be ready to serve the judicial function of a Limited World Government. However, these courts currently are backed by no means of enforcing their decisions and setting forth penalties, a deficiency that would be remedied by creation of an empowered Global Parliament, an Executive Council and a Global Peace Force.

4. INDEPENDENT SOURCE OF REVENUE. To support its own operations and a Global Peace Force, the Limited World Government must have a dependable and direct source of revenue so it will not be hostage to any national government for its operational funds. This has been a chronic problem with the UN.

As a source of direct revenue to the UN, taxes could be levied on any of several international corporate or individual transactions, currency exchanges or travel. Other possible revenue sources are listed in <u>Appendix D</u>. Except perhaps for a miniscule personal income tax on individuals with comfortable incomes, it is important that revenue sources for a Limited World Government not compete with the usual sources of national governments.

Until adequate revenue sources becomes a reality the Limited World Government will have to operate "on credit" from member governments and financial institutions.

5. INDEPENDENT "GLOBAL POLICE FORCE". To enforce edicts of the Global Parliament and to fulfill other duties, the Limited World Government must have an independent "Global Peace Force". This force must be made up of volunteers from member nations and be under the command of a world government general staff. Its command structure must be independent from that of any nation. The volunteer "Global Peace Force" will need special training and up-to-date equipment and to be at peak readiness at all times.

In addition to routine border patrols and other peace keeping commitments assigned by the Global Parliament or the Executive Council, the Global Peace Force must be ready to enforce Global Parliament, ICJ and ICC rulings against countries or individuals who have broken global laws. With equipment and specially trained personnel, Global Peace Force units also would be ready and available to assist anywhere in the world in rescue operations and natural catastrophes, such as the December 2004 South Asia tsunami.

How large should such a force be? Others have proposed forces from 60,000 to 400,000 troops. Perhaps a force of 100,000 individuals would be adequate as a target to establish such a force, which would be organized into several specialized units. They would have up-to-date equipment and have units stationed in several places throughout the world with aircraft and land equipment to permit high mobility. No nuclear weapons, depleted uranium projectiles, or land mines would be permitted.

As member nations disarm, equipment from national military stockpiles and training technologists might become available at little or no cost. The Global Peace Force also might gain recruits from reduced national military forces.

6. DISARMAMENT. Disarmament must take place so the massive world-wide inventory of military equipment and personnel can be reduced. This reduction and a reduction in military budgets would make large sums of money available

for important infrastructure and "people" uses, and to support world government efforts in TLA countries. In addition, "the people", through their governments, need to reassert their power over the military-industrial industry itself. However, disarmament and shifting of military budgets can not happen until nations are confident there is in place a reliable alternative to provide for the nation's "security".

Of all countries in the world, disarmament will be especially difficult for the United States because it has become so deeply involved with the military since World War II. The United States has more armaments and investments in military technology than most of the rest of the world combined. Hundreds of military bases are scattered around the world, thousands of businesses produce military equipment or provide other services, while hundreds of communities depend on the military as their primary employer.

One suggestion for managing disarmament is for each nation to reduce its military budget, equipment inventory and personnel by 10% (from its present standing) each year for a decade. Even if nations were willing to follow through on this proposal, it could not happen until other elements of a Limited World Government are in place, including an adequately equipped Global Peace Force that will have proved its readiness to handle difficult confrontations between nations.

It is fortunate that a tested alternative is available that might reduce some opposition from those whose livelihood depends heavily on the military. Switzerland, Sweden, the British Labor Party and the German Social Democratic Party years ago adopted or endorsed the "non-offensive defense policy". This alternative has several names, but its essence is to emphasize homeland defense and give up nuclear arsenals and weapons most useful for offensive military actions.

This alternative is examined in Chapter 7 of Hollins et al, Conquest of War. (17) It offers a means by which individual countries can independently draw down their armaments and demonstrate to their neighbors and the world an abandonment of the capability for preemptive or offensive military actions. Nations adopting this strategy thereby leave to the new Limited World Government the responsibility for military and police actions to maintain world peace.

7. AID TO PEOPLE. And finally to the last essential for a viable Limited World Government: To be successful, the new Limited World Government must have functions that go beyond a "World Parliament", chief executive and

executive council, a court system, independent funding, a "Global Peace Force", and disarmament.

The Limited World Government also must have the power and the assets to assist in reducing poverty and improving the lives of ordinary people. Part I included three quotations that called attention to the "Revolution of Rising Expectations". Those quoted said that if wealthier nations did not help improve the lives of those in poverty that great disruption and terrorism was likely to ensue. I followed those with Sir Peter Ustinov's perceptive quote about war and terrorism.

In 1961 Professor and Dean Paul Shipman Andrews recommended a course of action by which the UN might be strengthened and world peace achieved. Crucial among his recommendations was this essential that also is needed for any successful Limited World Government:

> "There must also be a World Mutual Development Fund....disposing annually of very large sums which, applied in wise and constructive projects, in areas in the course of development, will gradually raise the standard of living of their peoples and give them hope." (18)

Notice especially that last point: to give them hope! Note also Shipman proposed that an agency of the UN, a "World Mutual Development Fund", should dispense "very large sums" for development of TLA areas. Helping all of the world's people toward lives of dignity, with good health and basic education should not be done grudgingly or simply to avert terrorism. These things should be done as matters of the heart and as expressions of our common humanity.

For decades better-off nations have used foreign aid as an element of their foreign policy. The United States loans or grants billions of dollars a year to particular nations in the hope of maintaining friendly relations. Too often, part of this aid has been in the form of military equipment or training, and although is facilitates reducing inventory of older military equipment, it does not help toward a more peaceful world. Too often foreign aid deals also are made to favor trade with American corporations.

Even sums representing only one per cent of each of the better-off countries' GDP would be more than three times the present level of giving or lending by TA nations to others. This function of a strengthened UN or a Limited World

Government through its many agencies and programs would replace the "foreign aid" nations now dispense on a bilateral basis to other nations.

Already the UN has several agencies whose mission is to assist TLA nations in their health, education, birth control and other development programs. Among these are the WHO, UNESCO, UNICEF and the FAO. It is assumed that these agencies and others would continue to carry out their functions under a reformed UN or a new Limited World Government.

A "Global Marshall Plan" has been mentioned as a humane way to use the "Peace Dividend". A "Peace Dividend" will follow significant reductions in military spending around the world, and that "dividend" should not be returned to the people. It must be used to fulfill the backlog of needs that have been passed over for decades because of our love affair with the military. Part of the "Peace Dividend" in each country also must be used to pay down national indebtedness. Management of a "Global Marshall Plan" or a "World Mutual Development Fund" using Peace Dividend monies should be done only through world government agencies, not by individual countries.

Intelligent use of Peace Dividend monies on education, health care, birth control, and infrastructure in TA as well as TLA countries could do more to help people, especially children, and stabilize the world than all the monies we have been spending on the military. Using a Peace Dividend wisely, to serve people and not giant corporations—and not with tax breaks mostly for the wealthy, will give hope to the people, will help cool the fires of terrorism and will empower people's movements toward democracy. If we really believe in helping spread democracy to those who do not have it, this is the way, the only way!

Obviously, to accomplish all of this the Limited World Government would need the support of the people of its member nations. Member nations must transfer to the new world government a portion of their Peace Dividend savings to be used to help the poorer among the world's people.

The key is to educate people to accept that we all are "world citizens" and that it is only through acknowledging our world citizenship that many of our most serious problems can be addressed.

E. THREE WAYS TO ACHIEVE A LIMITED WORLD GOVERNMENT

Any problem that can be identified has a solution, although the solutions to some problems might need new technologies and institutions that do not exist. It is obvious that this writer believes a Limited World Government is the only solution to the major problems facing the world at this time and that we can begin working toward it now.

With advances in computers, communications and travel Limited World Government can be managed and financed. And perhaps most important of all: It will work when people demand it and are willing to support it as a better way toward their security.

Assuming that with the evidence presented, political scientists, sociologists, financial experts, educational psychologists, politicians, statesmen and others will acknowledge the urgency of taking action on the critical issues, it will be up to those experts to develop and implement strategies and steps to achieve a viable Limited World Government. As a geographer, a United States citizen and world citizen, I can only point in a general way toward that achievement. And, as the threat of terrorism recedes, peaceful living in a world without war and with violence reduced will rejuvenate the human spirit and bring on an age of cooperation, inventiveness and progress, as the threat of terrorism recedes.

Even though the new central government would have LIMITED functions and powers its powers must be adequate to fulfill the goals of that new world government or the effort would be futile. And member nations or a group of nations, once having joined, should not have the option of withdrawing in the future.

Over the decades many individuals have presented ideas and plans for a successful world government. Doubtless there are many ways by which a Limited World Government might be achieved. Three ways are presented here. The

FIRST and most direct way is by member nations amending the United Nations Charter. Only a few key changes in the UN's organization, funding and power—if they could be agreed upon—could make it an effective "world government".

The SECOND is for individuals representing each nation to meet and develop a world constitution, which—if there was enough support from "the people"—their governments (hopefully) would ratify, thus setting in motion formation of a Limited World Government.

The THIRD way is for the governments of the world's democracies—or representatives of the people of countries with democratic governments—to develop a Constitution and form a Limited World Government that at first would include only a few dozen of the world's nations, but the door would be open for others to join as they, too, become democracies.

1. MODIFY THE UNITED NATIONS. Organizationally the simplest and most direct means of achieving Limited World Government would be to amend the United Nations Charter. To function as a Limited World Government, a revised United Nations would need to be structured to include the seven characteristics cited in the preceding section.

This could be done within the present organization of the UN without going back to "square one" and drafting a new Charter. Several of those quoted have said if the United States WILL LEAD in helping to build a new world government structure above the nations, our country and all the good it represents will be remembered for all time as a beacon on the hill! If the United States would lead in strengthening the UN and offer to give up the veto, other veto holding nations may follow.

However, considering the United States' enormous power and the negative attitude of the current United States administration toward the UN, it is acknowledged that this alternative toward Limited World Government does not appear to be realistic, at least for the next few years. This is unfortunate because since its inception about two-thirds of United States citizens have supported the UN and many would like to see it strengthened. But things can change at election time. Several of those quoted in this book have said as much.

As with the UN, for a new Limited World Government to be successful, United States citizens must carry the largest share of the financial burden, at least during its early years. Keep in mind that for decades United States taxpayers and those in other countries have been paying large sums in a vain search for security through military might. We need to as willing to pay substantially for waging peace!

Over the years many individuals have put forth ideas for modifying the UN so it might function as a Limited World Government. Some are mentioned in the paragraphs that follow; others are in <u>Appendices C, D, E and F</u>.

Grenville Clarke and Louis B. Sohn are among those who developed a plan for modifying the UN Charter so the UN could have more power and begin to function as a world government. Their plan was written in 1958. Key points in their proposal are cited in <u>Appendix E1</u>. Henry B. Hollins and others examined in detail the Clarke and Sohn proposal for a "World Peacekeeping Federation" in Chapter 4 of their 1989 book, <u>Conquest of War</u>. (19)

In a plan he calls "The Catalyst", George Rosenfeld proposed in 1982 another process by which the UN might be modified so it would be able to fulfill its primary purpose of controlling disputes between nations. His plan begins with UN representatives going back to their home countries with the charge that each develop a set of proposed laws and UN amendments they would accept (as changes in the UN Charter) to make the world safe from major conflicts. According to Rosenfeld's proposal, a UN special committee would then be formed to develop from these proposals from individual UN member nations a "common denominator" plan acceptable to all. (20) As interesting as is this proposal, its coalescing process is likely to yield a minimal set of proposed amendments that would fall short of the several key items needed to make the UN a viable Limited World Government.

The title of Benjamin Ferencz's mid-1990s book, <u>New Legal Foundations For Global Survival: Security Through the Security Council</u>, indicates his conclusion. His scholarly and well documented book focuses on efforts that have taken place this century toward eliminating war and presents an array of quotes along with analysis of legalistic efforts that have been tried and found wanting. His conclusion is that security can be found through UN Charter changes made by the Security Council.

After considering and setting aside many approaches toward world government, Ferencz accepts and develops President Clinton's September 1993 suggestion that the UN could be made more functional and efficient by the Security Council's adoption of twelve resolutions: five to define legal obligations of members essential to maintaining peace; three to empower international judicial organs; and four to set up agencies to enforce peace mandates. Although he acknowledges that sovereignty is no longer an issue, Ferencz is concerned about a "balance of power" among the UN's agencies. Ferencz does not question retention of the veto and the domination of the UN by its largest and strongest members. (21) Further, I found nothing in his book about the need for an independent revenue source for the UN.

In 1994 Harold Stassen, former Governor of Minnesota and participant in the (1945) San Francisco Conference that gave birth to the UN, wrote a detailed proposal for modifying the UN Charter. Stassen presents several interesting ideas, including several for an independent revenue source for the UN. However, he, too, would retain the veto and did not propose a world government. He proposed, instead that the UN become "an improved center of cooperation between sovereign governments." (22) Key elements of his plan are listed in Appendix E2. Perhaps he was convinced major nations would not go beyond his limited level of changes.

In days long gone kings, sultans, maharajahs, and czars insisted their powers were given to them and their families by God. They and their dukes, barons, pashas, scherifs and their like wielded the power of life and death over peasants, serfs, slaves, vassals, and scullions who did their bidding, fought their wars and paid taxes for the royal establishment. The peasants were unschooled and were thought to be unfit to participate in governance.

But note that in a way the UN is now organized as in the days of old. Leaders of only a few of the world's most powerful countries, like the kings of old, hold tight to the strings of power in the Security Council. Even the 101 reforms presented by Kofi Annan's committee in late 2004 recommend a Security Council enlarged to 24 with rotating members added but with the veto retained. The reform suggestions do not address the issue of the UN's lack of power, its need for a direct source of income, and the reform suggestions include nothing to rectify significantly the powerlessness of the smaller nations or the General Assembly.

The smaller nations even now have very little voice in UN decisions and workings. They continue to support the UN and its larger purposes because there is no other game in town that gives them a forum to at least present their concerns. And they do benefit greatly from services offered by the UN's many agencies.

And finally, in 1958 H. B. Hollins, editor of the booklet quoted in the Introduction (and at the end of this book), after reviewing the total cost of military expenditures of all nations, presented a plan for amending the UN

Charter so it would function as a Limited World Government. Hollins' five "Financial Facts", his three part plan and steps to be taken by the UN (under Charter Article 108) are included as <u>Appendix E3</u>. Making the initial steps to amend the UN Charter so it could function as a world government can be started by the UN General Assembly where the veto does not apply. However, final approval must include nations that hold the veto power.

Modifying the UN Charter, therefore, would be the most direct way to achieve a Limited World Government, but, at least for now, blockage is likely to come mainly from nations holding the veto power, including the United States.

2. WORLDWIDE "PEOPLE'S INITIATIVE". If key members of the UN Security Council and others will not support action to modify the UN by amending its Charter to achieve a Limited World Government, another way must be implemented.

After identifying self-evident truths and the right of every individual to Life, Liberty and the pursuit of Happiness, our Declaration of Independence acknowledges the people's right to form new government if their government is not providing those rights. As Ferenz said, "if leaders won't lead, let the people lead, and the leaders will surely follow." (23) Garry Davis also encourages individuals who acknowledge their "world citizenship" to organize a world government and then seek legitimization of the new world government through their national governments. Clearly, as President Eisenhower said, it IS time for governments "to get out of the way and let the people have peace"!

On December 10, 1948, the UN adopted the "Universal Declaration of Human Rights", a document similar to our Declaration of Independence and Bill of Rights. Article 28 of the Declaration of Human Rights states specifically that all of the world's people are entitled to "social and international order". Accepting the usual meaning of the words in the phrase "social and international order", no nation by itself can fulfill that entitlement.

Acknowledging that much of the time many members of the human family have been at war and "without social and international order", acknowledging further the impotence of the UN as presently structured, representatives of the world's people could meet to take steps toward forming a Limited World Government to provide the order people yearn for as well as basic human rights. The "world's people" do not have to organize gargantuan meetings around the world to set this method of organizing a world government in motion. Small groups meeting in many places could be united in preliminary deliberations by Internetting and teleconferencing.

But then questions arise: Who should appoint or elect these representatives to a final constitutional convention, if one is needed, and whom will they represent? If one was needed, how large should such a conclave be to represent reasonably the world's people and still be manageable? And what would happen to constitution drafts or decisions made at such a meeting? How many people from how many countries exchanging ideas and developing consensus on a world constitution draft would be sufficient to gain the attention and support of enough national governments to bring ratification and a positive result?

With different kinds of governments and controlling interests, representatives chosen for a convention to draft a Constitution for a Limited World Government could be selected in a variety of ways. In countries with a strong democratic tradition representatives of the people could be chosen from among those already elected to high office. These could be supplemented with individuals chosen because of their demonstrated support of the people in many different contexts and organizations.

However, most of the approximately 200 national governments around the world are not really democratic. Many have elections but only a façade of democracy. Behind the scenes the control of many governments remains with strong military, corporate and or religious interests that also dominate the media and distort elections. (It is very troubling, but in recent years, with heavy corporate and religious involvement in our elections and our government, the United States shows signs of slipping into being a "façade democracy".)

In countries without a democratic tradition selection of representatives could pose a problem.

Non-democratic governments might participate in a Limited World Government with the ulterior motive of putting a "human face" on their regimes, even as they continue to repress the people. Individual citizens from countries living under an authoritarian boot who might want to participate in an organizing convention are not likely to be selected by an autocratic government.

If "self-selected" individuals were able to attend meetings at their own initiative and expense, they should be permitted to do so. They would present themselves as world citizens who want to participate in any way they can. That, too, should be acceptable because the convention would want to use all talent and commitment available to further the formation of a viable Limited World Government. Furthermore, the conference would be self-organizing and would choose leaders from all who attend who could best support the interests of all in achieving a viable Limited World Government that would have powers *not* granted to the UN. Further, the meetings would be carried on with democratic procedures so the meeting itself would educate non-democratic governments as to some of the norms of a democracy and civilized society.

Although one can hope the United States would participate wholeheartedly in meetings and the formation of a new world government—and then join, there can be no guarantee. Just as was said about giving up the veto power in the UN, joining a proposed world government would entail member nations giving some powers to the new world government to achieve "social and international order" that was not forthcoming from their military investments. Most nations in the world wield little power on the world scene and would be inclined to join a Limited World Government. Although, depending on how it was presented, most people in the United States might be inclined to join a Limited World Government, the government, with its power and dominance, might be opposed.

However, if most countries were to organize a Limited World Government— even without the United States—its power compared to the United States would be overwhelming in everything except military power. Perhaps some would support it to counter the dominance of the United States and its multinational corporations. There could be intense friction between such a fledgling Limited World Government and the United States government and its major corporations. However, by the peaceful power and economic success of such a Limited World Government, the people of the United States and any other "hold-out" nation would find it in their best interest to elect those who would abandon special agendas and begin cooperating with others.

3. "FEDERATED WORLD DEMOCRACIES" (FWD). As suggested by Ronald Glossop, Lionel Curtis and others, a joining of the people of the world's truly democratic nations to form a world government would be another and perhaps the most promising way to achieve a Limited World Government. Such a joining of nations would be an immediate formidable player on the world scene, again with or without the United States. Democracies already have traditions and mechanisms in place to choose representatives for such an endeavor. An important question, "When and how would a transition be made from the UN to a FWD?", will be taken up later.

Acknowledging that many democracies are sham democracies or façade democracies, what countries would be given the green light to participate in the formation of and become members of a new FWD? And who should judge what country is a true democracy and what is not?

Four criteria are suggested here as litmus tests for a democracy: embracing human rights in word and deed, establishing fair elections that include women (and this would include fair and open vote counting, with peaceful transition to an opposing party!), having a truly "free press" (including all media and not dominated by the government) that takes seriously its obligation to keep the electorate truthfully informed, and accepting the rule of law, including codifications that have been accepted as international law—like the Geneva Conventions on Prisoners of War and other treaties that have been established on behalf of the Earth's people.

The experience of democratic nations joining together for a purpose is demonstrated in the beginnings of the United States, the Allies during World War II, and the evolution of the European Union and NATO. The European Union is on its way—slowly to be sure—to equal the United States in its power and influence as one of the world's large democratic unions. NATO, with 23 European member nations plus Canada, the United States and Turkey, is another model of an organization of democratic nations that supercedes the nations themselves. NATO was organized in 1949 specifically to keep the peace between Western Europe and the Soviet Union and its Eastern Europe allies. In recent years NATO has taken on expanded responsibilities in Afghanistan.

But then what body should decide which nations measure up to the litmus test standards of being a democracy? This sensitive but important task should be undertaken by an impartial panel of world judges, and I can think of no better group that the International Court of Justice in the Netherlands.

Depending on an honest appraisal of a nation's true "people characteristics", only several dozen nations are likely to qualify as "democracies" for participation in a convention to form a Federation of World Democracies. Representatives from non-democratic nations should be welcome to attend as non-voting observers with the opportunity to express their views and make suggestions.

It also is important to note that the few dozen democratic nations that might form a "Federated World Democracies" even now control most of the world's wealth and technological development. These nations also hold the power strings of the UN and have overwhelming military power.

These facts alert us to several questions. With their past, and since they still dominate the world, will representatives of these more advanced democratic countries propose a constitution and organize a Limited World Government that truly would serve the interests of *all* of the world's people on into the future? Or will their constitution be self-serving and continue their dominance in some way?

Will the non-democratic nations and people who are not in on the formation of a Federated World Democracies accept the legitimacy of that new government with its "open door" to possible membership if they jump several hoops to be accepted as "democracies"? After all, TLA countries, many of them non-democratic, have jumped difficult hoops for their "mother countries" in years past and more recently for the World Bank and IMF in efforts to qualify for loans "to develop". Many have struggled to pay off these loans with over half of their export earnings, with social programs languishing, and they are still desperately behind in payments.

Further, is it "undemocratic" or "elitist" to even contemplate forming a world government limited to "democracies"? How could such a new "Federated World Democracies" function if only approximately one third of the world's nations and people comprise the first group of members? Doesn't organizing a federation of the world's democracies fly in the face of the increasing "interdependence of all nations and people"?

And there are additional questions. If world government were to be achieved through a Federated World Democracies or another way, what would happen to the UN? With the formation of a FWD would the democracies of the world withdraw from the UN? Without the support of nations with the strongest economies would the UN wither and be forced to discontinue many of its many functions? How long would it take a new Federated World Democracies to gain standing as a world organization and have the authority to mount peacekeeping actions through its new "Global Peace Force"? Until many more nations joined the FWD, how would the work of the UN's world-embracing agencies relate to a limited membership FWD? Would a reduced UN continue on and become primarily the instrument and voice of developing TLA nations as they seek to democratize and improve their situations?

All of these are pertinent questions and there can be no clear answers. As was mentioned, from the beginning of a "Federated World Democracies" the door must be open for representatives of all nations to have "associate membership" and the privilege to participate in discussions, but no vote.

As we embark on the rocky but necessary road to world government in these early years of the twenty first century we should do so without looking back and without being encumbered by many terrible injustices that happened, some going back hundreds of years. As idealistic as this may seem, it must be taken seriously if the human family is to avoid serious disruption during the next decades. We must abandon old cultural baggage and move ahead with faith in the good will and intelligence of those who meet to organize a fair FWD, with nothing hidden, a viable world government that will serve the world's people on into the future.

If representatives of the democracies fail in this, those left out might organize their own super-government of disadvantaged "left-out nations". Or perhaps the UN itself would become that vehicle. If hope is left languishing, some of the "left out" might slip back into terrorism.

The same two options that were explained for implementing a "World Wide Peoples' Initiative" also would apply to a FWD. The simplest and most direct way would be for the governments of a group of the world's democratic nations, representing their "sovereign" people, to appoint or elect representatives to draft a constitution for a FWD, which their governments would ratify to bring the new FWD into existence.

However, if leaders of democratic governments are slow to take action to initiate a Global Constitutional Convention, representatives of the "people" can call such an enclave as our colonial forebears did in 1787, when the Constitution was hammered out and the Articles of Confederation were set aside. Would the governments of democracies interfere while peaceful meetings are held to discuss and possibly plan for a Limited World Government? If the answer is "no", these are true democracies. If a "democratic" government would interfere with such meetings, it is not a true democracy.

Drafts of proposed World Constitutions already exist. One such draft was proposed in 1948 by (then) Chancellor Robert Hutchins of the University of Chicago and other scholars. Key elements of their proposed world constitution are summarized in Appendix F. Others also have proposed drafts of world government constitutions through the years.

To facilitate its consideration and approval by member nations, a proposed Constitution for a "Federated World Democracies" must be as short and succinct as possible. It must reaffirm a Declaration of Human Rights. It must establish a balance among its several parts to assure that no tyrant can take over on behalf of an open or secret agenda. It must include the 7 essential elements that were presented in the preceding section. Furthermore, the manner by which it could be amended must be clear, and a formal review of the Constitution should be undertaken every twenty years to consider possible modifications.

Ratification of a world constitution document acceptable to the sovereign people in each nation will come when the people have convinced their government that joining the new world organization will be a direct and long term benefit to the people of that nation as a whole. Ratification will not come easily or quickly, as France and the Netherlands demonstrated in early 2005 with their "no" votes on the proposed Constitution for the European Union.

Ratification will come only when candidates and legislators in democratic countries realize that to be elected or reelected they must follow the peoples' wishes to join the new world government. The people of Connecticut showed us how in November 1948! It is a challenge to them to be first again! Or will the people of Illinois or another state show the way?

How long would it take to establish a new world-level government, a "Federated World Democracies"? Our experience with formation of the UN in only a few months at the close of World War II is one possibility. The half century development of the European Union is another.

However, considering the urgency of the issues we face and with the tremendous power of modern electronic and communication technologies at hand, establishing a "Federated World Democracies" or FWD must not require a half century. In fact, Western civilization and the world will be in deep trouble if it were to take that long.

With the FWD model, important changes will come as non-democratic (mostly TLA) nations democratize and become full members and as the new world government proves itself in preventing war and helping people around the world live more satisfying lives. When these things happen all nations will seek membership in the new FWD and that new organization will be acknowledged as the world organization that should replace the UN itself.

4. CONCLUSION. It would be expected that a "Federated World Democracies" or a Limited World Government, regardless how it came to be, from its start would work with the UN and perhaps from its offices. It would be further expected that many UN staff members would continue on in the new world government. Also, the many specialized UN agencies would continue their usual functions, but under a new umbrella.

When you get right down to it, the simplest way to achieve world government in our time is for members of the UN, especially with the United States leading the way, to make the Charter changes that are needed to transform that organization into a Limited World Government. The draft of the UN Charter came into being after only three months of intense deliberations (August to October 1944) largely by representatives of the world's major democracies. It could be done again to develop a Limited World Government.

A critical question was raised at the end of Part II: By what means is it possible, even with an empowered Limited World Government, to control the activities of multi-national corporations that now operate in a world of international anarchy, a world with few if any international restraints? Or, to ask the question in an obverse way: How can the actions of multi-national corporations be made more humane? It could be done through a Limited World Government that had the power to levy taxes and impose penalties. But it must be emphasized: This could be done only if the world's people insist and strongly back a Limited World Government that has been given the needed powers.

Regardless of which alternative is adopted to achieve a Limited World Government, it is time to face our critical problems squarely and seek solutions that have the best chance of leading us to a more just and secure future for ourselves, but mostly for our children. Our history and the world's history can inform us and help us as we choose what to do and what not to do.

If we are to achieve a better world for our children and those who follow, the most important change must come in our hearts and minds. We *must* do things that will enhance the lives of all people, not just ourselves. Changes must give every family some chance of improvement, especially for the children. Changes should not further aggrandize or enrich corporations, CEOs, or particular national governments.

We *must* do better than those who came before and our own generations have done so far in solving problems reasonably. And whatever we do, we must do it with fairness and justice—without rancor or violence—to unlock untold opportunities for our children and those who follow in all parts of the world.

F. OPPOSITION TO LIMITED WORLD GOVERNMENT

It is easy to find fault with a program or agency, and some folks are good at criticism. It is always easier to tear down than to build. It is not easy look beyond one's immediate situation and make suggestions for the common good of a community, whether that "community" is one's home town, a state, a nation or the world. That is the challenge of today.

The word "attitude" has crept into our vocabulary in recent years with a new meaning. A person is said to have an "attitude" if he or she insists on doing things "his way" or "her way" or simply to be noticed, probably with not much thought of others. "Attitude" tends to be a "me first" or "my way" word, and unfortunately in recent years it reflects too much the way many citizens live their lives and also the arrogant "go it alone" foreign policy of some govern-ments, including ours in Washington.

Over a half century ago when I was a fledgling geography professor at Florida State University we taught that "attitude" should be considered a "cultural resource" for or against progress. A "positive attitude" of a people or country could lead to innovation and improvement, the acceptance of useful change and progress. Positive attitudes include a willingness to cooperate with others to make needed changes, a feeling of responsibility for the community at large, and other forward-looking attributes. Negative attitudes could be a fierce pro-tection of the status quo, a belligerence toward changes and persons outside their group, and the inability to face and deal with problems or opportunities at hand.

Opposition to a Limited World Government will come from many different quarters. Those in TA areas may oppose Limited World Government for fear that TLA areas with their growing populations would dominate the Earth and a new world government in a few years. On the other hand, TLA areas might oppose Limited World Government out of fear that TA areas would try to force birth control and otherwise "lock in" their current domination. Opposition also is likely from other individuals and groups, as noted on the following pages. However, the facts about the critical and urgent challenges we must face will stand even as some may oppose a Limited World Government as a viable solution.

1. OPPOSITION FROM THE MILITARY. Many individuals in corporations and communities whose primary support is the military are likely to oppose a Limited World Government because they do not believe a Limited World Government will provide the level of "security" the military now provides. Or they may oppose Limited World Government because it would bring on major changes in their lives. Those serving in the military and who actually may be put in "harm's way" are likely to have mixed feelings about a new approach that could bring peace. As much as their livelihood would be affected most surely they would prefer to live in peace with their families. Of course, when disarmament begins some who want to continue with military careers could join the Global Peace Force that was described.

Objections from those in the military, in military communities, in businesses with military contracts, and those in security positions, though important, become hollow when long term peace and stability are in the balance.

Humans have been going through this war cycle for so many millennia that making war appears to be normal human behavior. As we have shown, it is not. Humans simply have been unwilling to do and pay for what is needed to "wage peace". Through our taxes each United States citizen pays about $1600 each year to the Pentagon for "security", but only $1.11 per person to the United Nations! We should put our money where it can bring the results we want!

Although not civilized or humane, war can be understood in times long gone before nations were so interdependent and before the technology was at hand for people to communicate so easily. The antidote to the war system is a global system of laws and justice secured through a Limited World Government. Such a system could for the first time on a world scale permit human ingenuity to flower.

An intelligent society will work toward that better way even as it acknowledges the many dislocations that will have to be resolved over the few decades in implementing a war-free world. The "Peace Dividend", money saved for other government uses from reductions in the military in almost every country, should not be given away as a tax refund. Such monies should be diverted to the long overdue attention to rebuilding infrastructure and schools and health facilities. It should be used to pay down government indebtedness and for job retraining and other programs to assist communities and individuals with the transition. New needs in a peaceful world will require retrained workers with many new and old skills

2. OPPOSITION FROM "LIFE STYLE". In the last forty years of so there has been a great change in the attitude and interests of many people. Surely things have changed in expanding human rights (until the Patriot Act) and how we communicate. There also have been great changes in the lifestyles and interests of many people, especially in the United States.

Some may oppose a Limited World Government because they focus on the here and now and want no one to rock the boat of their life style. Many folks have developed a fixation on games, TV entertainment, races, fast foods and consumerism. They are "political" but not many take the trouble to vote. They seem to accept everything the government says as truth. Those with these interests and attitude ignore the future consequences of a narrow "me first" and "keeping up with the Joneses" life style. Are they unchangeable?

I don't think so. Changes in attitude, along with parallel changes in our economy, have taken place in only a few decades. I believe in the power of truthful education. Ill-serving and erroneous ideas that have been learned can be set aside as evidence is presented to show a better way. Regardless of one's lifestyle, we all want our children to have a reasonable chance at happiness and fulfillment during their lives.

We must relearn a concern for our communities. We can learn or relearn realities about our Earth, our neighbors on this planet, and what will happen if basic problems are left unattended.

3. OPPOSITION FROM "THE POWERFUL". Most who hold positions of power in the world's economic and governmental systems are likely to oppose initiatives toward a Limited World Government. These would include many members of Congress and office holders at all levels of government, as well as CEOs and high level staff of major and minor corporations and businesses, especially multinational corporations.

These individuals are likely to oppose changes toward a Limited World Government because of the many uncertainties in our transition from the present war-based system to a war-free world. They may oppose Limited World Government because of the unknowns as to what a war-free world would offer them as "positions of power" in the new world. Those in multinational corporations may oppose Limited World Government because of fees and taxes that are likely to be imposed to control those corporations and to provide revenue for the new world government.

Some persons with power in the world's governments also may oppose Limited World Government because of the "sovereignty issue". The granting of any part of the people's "sovereignty" is seen as a step not to be taken. However, these individuals need to be reminded that already, in our interdependent and partially globalized economy, sovereignty is a tired old myth. People need to be reminded that it is their right to organize government to provide "social and international order". Nations usurped the peoples' sovereignty and then have been giving it up bit by bit to gigantic corporations as globalization has been taking place.

In too many cases individuals who are elected to the United States House of Representatives or Senate go to Washington expecting to do great things to help the American people. In Washington they immediately become enmeshed in the race for reelection, they are hounded by lobbyist after lobbyist, and the shine of their idealism is dimmed. They become bogged down in a sluggish "go with the flow" and "business as usual" approach that in recent years character-izes Washington. Only a courageous few will come forward to provide the initiative and leadership needed to make changes toward a Limited World Government or a "Federated World Democracies". Most elected officials will wait until "the people" instruct them with their votes. So again it is "up to the people"!

4. OPPOSITION FROM FUNDAMENTALISTS. Some of the most "funda-mental" Christians view the violent and problem-ridden world as the beginning throes of "Armageddon". They believe the world soon will be coming to a sudden and violent end. The "saved" will go to heaven, sinners to hell, and there is no long-term future to be concerned about.

Over the centuries "Armageddon" has been predicted many times by funda-mentalist leaders. Yet the Universe continues in its dramatic ways and the world continues its annual revolution around the sun. Cosmologists tell us it will continue for another five billion years or so. Apart from the possibility of another asteroid striking the Earth, life forms will continue on Earth for eons. Whether and how the human experiment on this planet continues is up to us, with the exciting possibility of some day contacting intelligent life forms on other planets, who surely are "out there".

It is my hope that the vast majority of adherents to all religions will apply the best of their religious values to achieve a war-free world with justice and peace under law. Opposition from fundamental extremists will simply have to be ignored.

5. OPPOSITION FROM "THE ELEPHANT IN THE ROOM". Some opposition to a Limited World Government also may be engendered when we acknowledge the "elephant in the room" that no one wants to talk about. What is "the elephant in the room"? The implementation of a just and fair Limited World Government is likely to lead over time to some leveling of incomes among the world's people. In his latest book, The World Is Flat, Thomas Friedman says a "flattening" or leveling of incomes in the world already is taking place. (24) If that is so, it is hardly noticeable.

However, with a worldwide leveling over time higher incomes in wealthier nations are likely to be reduced somewhat; lower incomes in poorer nations will be edging up. This leveling of incomes is the "elephant in the room" that is ignored in discussions about "corporate globalization", "enlightened globalization" and world government.

As the issue is analyzed, however, many will see that there is a reasonable trade-off. To gain a peaceful and fairer world those with higher incomes must accept a possible modest reduction in income, but more counter-balancing positive results will be gained in this trade-off, as I will explain!

We in the "Western" world must realize further that our whole culture and way of life has been "built on sand" in at least two ways. FIRST, like a drug-dependent teenager, the economies and citizens in many countries (not only the TA nations) depend on an obsessive "petroleum fix", and no government has come forward with a serious plan to break that dependency even though relatively cheap petroleum will last only a few decades. It is this need and obsession with petroleum that has driven United States foreign policy for decades and makes us look to the Middle East that owns most of the world's reserves. The United States' ownership of half of the world reserves of oil shale will at most add only a few more decades to our petroleum addiction when development of that resource becomes profitable.

And SECOND, the affluent way of life most "Westerners" enjoy is deeply dependant on poorly paid workers on the bottom of our own and the world's economic system. Let's admit it: the colonial world of the past is gone, but today's world operates with "economic colonialism", and the United States is its leader. We are leading this "economic colonialism" through the policies of the

World Bank, IMF and WTO, which do not help TLA countries develop. And "economic colonialism" is one of the forces driving terrorists.

With our declining employment, jobs going overseas, the trade deficit ballooning, a rapidly growing national debt, the growing chasm between rich and poor on our planet, and on top of all that add global warming, a day of reckoning is coming for our Western way of life. Disruptions to our Western way of life will not come as Armageddon—a sudden end to all with everyone wearing a "Sorting Hat" and being sent to heaven or hell. Unless we change our ways it will come instead as a new "Dark Age" is thrust upon us. Wars will increase, democracies will die, and the lives of most on this planet are likely to be disrupted, limited and difficult for decades.

Those who oppose Limited World Government because of the "elephant in the room" are misguided because these disruptions will be coming even if little or nothing is done now! A Limited World Government should be supported because it can at least put us on the road to solving our critical problems that can only be solved on a global basis. By instituting a Limited World Government we might forestall and perhaps set aside disruptions such as those mentioned that are on the horizon.

The important aspect of the trade-off I mentioned is that a modest reduction in income and in our national GDP (Gross Domestic Product) over a decade or two would not necessarily mean a reduction in QUALITY of day to day living for any of us! Let me repeat that because it is so important: A modest reduction in income and in our national GDP (Gross Domestic Product) over a decade or two would not necessarily mean a reduction in QUALITY of day to day living for any of us!

There will be dislocations of workers and communities as military facilities and military related businesses are closed. If the issue of a world community in peace were left to military-minded individuals and businesses, wars would never cease because new "enemies" can always be hyped and more powerful new military machines would be invented and used in endless years of more wars.

On the other hand, with controlled globalization in a world community we can expect many new business and employment opportunities and new inventions to provide goods and services for a more humane and developing world. But these things can happen *only* if levels of living are raised in most parts of the Earth and new markets are opened.

Besides saving money with reduced military costs and adopting more intelligent ways to use energy, we could save money in two more ways that in the long run would improve our children and grandchildren's lives. Bruce Bower said in a <u>Science News</u> article: "Modern citizens are consumed by life, liberty and the pursuit of more and better stuff, prodded on by the relentless flow of advertisements designed to create a flood or retail desires." (25)

We in the West have been "binging" not only on petroleum but also on many of the Earth's resources. In fairness to others on this planet, we need to scale back our super-consumerism that is fueled by our endless super-advertising. By taming our hyper-advertising and over-indulgent materialism and by building things that will last longer we would save money and resources, we could reduce our vast wastage of food and energy, and we would need far fewer landfills for our trash!

Remember all of the "bad" things the GDP includes: financial losses from auto accidents, crimes, catastrophic and routine medical expenses, fire losses, legal expenses, etc.? Reductions in these through a universal health care system, by being less "driven", by "getting along with each other" and becoming a less litigious society, by getting at the economic fairness roots of our crime and imprisonment problem, and by adopting better nutrition habits actually could lead to improving our way of life and our happiness even with modestly reduced incomes.

Of course, those changes might lead to opposition from the food industry, the pharmaceutical industry, the insurance industry, and we would need fewer lawyers, etc. But we should be willing to deal with such opposition to find the peaceful world with justice that we seek.

Earlier the "Peace Dividend" was mentioned. Monies saved from sharply reduced military expenditures could be like winning the lottery, not for individuals directly, but for our communities, nation and world! As our military stockpiles, equipment, personnel and budgets are drawn down the "Peace Dividend" could be used to fulfill critical needs in the United States and abroad. We could support the Global Marshall Plan proposed by former Senator and Vice President Al Gore and others to address problems within the United States and to assist those in poorer countries of the world. Among the better off nations in the world the United States spends the least portion of its Gross Domestic Product on foreign aid, and much of that aid is for the military.

It was estimated a few years ago that for $40 billions per year over 20 years the world problems of health, nutrition and education could be resolved. That estimate did not include infrastructure and other economic development costs. No doubt it would cost several times that amount to accomplish that in these early years of the twentieth century. Even $120 billions each year for twenty years would be less than one third of our annual military budget! One hundred twenty billion dollars also is *about one-third of the INTEREST we pay each year on our national debt!*

Within the United States we could use funds from a Peace Dividend to help the needy among us and reduce our national debt and deficit and use the billions we pay each year in interest in more constructive ways. We could enhance health care, build schools and improve education. We could develop more job training centers, and improve streets, bridges and sewer facilities. There also would be enough, given the huge Pentagon budget which would then be greatly reduced, to shore up Medicare, Medicaid, and the Social Security trust fund!

Speaking only about the United States, the Peace Dividend clearly would be large enough to accomplish all of the domestic and foreign programs listed. We could do all of those things and more to improve the lives of people—in peace—in our own country and the world—without raising taxes! And, perhaps, after some years, when we have accomplished much, no longer have the military juggernaut to support, and have paid off our national debt, taxes in our country and others around the world might be reduced!

We obviously have been willing to pay our taxes through the years as we have unsuccessfully sought security through military might. We should be willing to pay taxes at similar rates for some more years to wage peace, reduce our national debt, help people and communities here and elsewhere in the world AND reduce the threat of terrorism!

The "Elephant in the Room" phenomenon can be a good thing if it will help us abandon attitudes that focus on self and our nation alone. We must replace such narrowing attitudes with positive feelings that put the whole world and all people under our umbrella of concern. Whatever religion each of us professes should help us become honestly and seriously concerned about others. By doing so we help ourselves, our children and those who follow to have a chance at a good life.

6. VOTER APATHY AND CYNICISM. The "status quo" of old-fashioned sovereignty has been broken. We all are living in a world undergoing massive

changes in every aspect of everyone's life: economic, religious, health care, family and governmental. Hundreds of thousands of jobs have been lost and lives already have been disrupted and altered in recent decades by the avalanche of changes in our communication technologies. Religious fundamentalists are pushing to remold governments to affirm their beliefs. Immigration policies and refugees are changing the face of many countries. Many have turned their backs on society, have stopped voting and have become hooked on sports and TV entertainment, or they are fearful of changes a "new world" might bring.

There have been other good reasons for voters in the United States to be cynical about their society and to have doubts about the political process. For many years our political process was dominated by political bosses and "smoke filled rooms". But the 2000 and 2004 national elections revealed more sinister problems. During these recent campaigns candidates and issues were cast in stark blacks and whites with much distortion and mud slinging. As is well known, the "winner" of the 2000 presidential campaign hung on results of the Florida election and was finally decided by the United States Supreme Court. The 2004 election hung on results from one state, Ohio, where the CEO of a voting machines factory guaranteed to "deliver" that state to the president. These elections do not speak well for our "democracy" and how every vote is supposed to be honestly counted.

Campaign reform is a must and the voting process by whatever means must be honest and subject to rechecking. Our election process should be shortened to a few months (to the dismay of the media!), and contributions to political campaigns should be made only by registered voters. With these changes those who are on the political sidelines might be able to put apathy and cynicism behind them as we all look ahead and become active participants in important decisions that must come soon.

7. THE VAST CHASMS. Some who oppose a Limited World Government bring up the vast cultural chasms that divide the world's people. They ask, "How can we ever hope to get together on an enterprise as large as a world government?" They say, "Maybe sometime in the future."

With monumental improvements in communication and transportation technologies in recent years, the simple issue of distance is no longer an obstacle to the world's people coming together and organizing a Limited World Government.

But the cultural and other chasms are very real. Apart from racial and ethnic differences, language differences and standards of living, we know cultural chasms include very different beliefs about many things. Some chasms stem from incidents in a long ago but not forgotten past. Many different beliefs have been deeply instilled by families, educational systems, religions and governments. Whether we acknowledge it or not or like the term, each of us has been "brain-washed" on many basic matters and feels that "our way" of doing things and what we believe is the right way.

We know from the decades of experience with the League of Nations and the UN that there are ways to work around the language barriers by using multiple languages and employing simultaneous translation. Since the late 1800s we know that Esperanto and its simplified Ido version offer "composite" languages that are relatively easy to learn and carry no baggage of originating with a particular nation or culture. As a matter of practicality we also realize that with computers and the Internet English is becoming a de facto world language.

We have shown that the world's major religions have a set of common values that can help us learn to cooperate with each other. We can not move into a more peaceful future unless we learn to get along with those who are different from us in many ways. Keep in mind that the DNA of every person is 99.9 per cent like that of every other person!

8. CONCLUSION. The globalization process is relentless and is taking advantage of the "chasms" that divide us. Many of the old ways of the world are now obsolete. A new world is being advanced by forces that will not stop. The question comes down simply to the kind of world we want to leave for our children: A world that continues the senseless and wasteful war system? A world that ignores basic problems that within a few decades will cause upheavals and compromise our democratic way of life? Or should we forge a new way, a way that, even with problems and dislocations in its birth, can set aside the war monster and offer hope and opportunity for each human being for all children for centuries to come?

Ronald Glossop, in his <u>World Federation? A Critical Analysis of Federal World Government</u>, presents a well documented and logical approach to change the minds of those who have some reason to oppose world government. His approach is to ask if the person would agree to give up government at national, state and/or local levels as we know them. If the answer is "yes", the individual is an anarchist or libertarian and no argument will sway him or her.

However, if the answer is "no", as most people would respond, ask the follow-up question "Why not?" The answer as to why we must have government and services at national, state or local levels is simply that these governments do important things for us that we can not do for ourselves. That same reasoning can be extended to support a government at the global level to perform needed services—like keeping the peace—which national governments have proved they cannot provide. (26)

Emery Reves, in his <u>Anatomy of Peace</u>, considers and refutes many of the arguments that might be made against world government. Perhaps the two paragraphs quoted below convey a most compelling question about how people respond to the concepts of war and peace:

> "It seems that the first and last maxim of national governments in quest of peace is 'All measures—short of law.' As peace is identical with law, it is not difficult to realize why we are no nearer our goal than we have been for centuries.
> "It is a mysterious characteristic of human nature that we are prepared to spend anything, to sacrifice everything, to give all we have and are when we wage war, and that we are never prepared to make more than an 'initial step,' make more than a 'first beginning,' adopt more than 'minimum measures,' when we seek to organize peace. When will our religions, our poets and our national leaders give up the lie that death is more heroic than life.?" (27)

Earlier I mentioned that Paul Simon was a strong advocate of the United Nations. He also was concerned that young people in general did not share that interest. Perhaps the lack of interest among young people in the UN and world issues stems from their view of the UN as an "old boys club" that simply can not do what it was designed to do: eliminate war involving the more powerful nations. Young people need a new banner under which to express their concerns about the world and their future! Perhaps that banner could be in support of a Limited World Government!

G. NINETEEN HOPEFUL SIGNS

Countering the several sources of probable opposition to a Limited World Government, there are many "hopeful signs" that signal the world is again ready for a revival of interest in a Limited World Government. Some of these are old, others are quite recent. A few have been mentioned elsewhere in this book; others have not. The nineteen items that follow, in no particular order, are items that support my optimism and hope.

1. Hopeful sign number one is the manner in which, over the last 150 years a growing number of world embracing institutions have been invented. The first group developed from the 1860s to World War I; the second group was added to the UN after its birth in 1945. Almost all of the earlier ones now also are affiliated with the UN. These agencies serve us all in our increasing worldwide interdependence. They are harbingers of the next logical and necessary step: a Limited World Government.

A key point here is that all of these international agencies and even the League of Nations and the UN are recent social inventions of mankind. New "inventions of social machinery" are not "born perfect". They are the result of a natural evolution in the progress of mankind as our ability to move about our planet and communicate have brought us to higher levels of interdependence—and new problems—and the need for a higher level of law in the world, "global law". If masses of people were keenly interested in world government after World War II, it can happen again!

2. The second hopeful sign is Emery Reves' book, The Anatomy of Peace [1946] and the widespread interest in World Government that followed World War II. Articles appeared during the 1940s and 1950s in many popular magazines explaining world government. Among these were articles in Woman's Day, The Rotarian, Fortune, Look, Saturday Review, Modern Industry, New Republic, and Common Cause.

More recently, I am buoyed by other books looking critically at war, including Hollins, Powers and Sommers' Conquest of War [1989], Ronald Glossop's Confronting War [1983, now in its 4th edition] and World Federation, A Critical Analysis of Federal World Government, [1993]. Glossop's books consider alternatives toward achieving world government, including a world "Federation of the Free" democratic nations.

3. A third hopeful sign is the progress that has been made, especially since World War II in the United States and the world, in the acceptance of basic human and civil rights for women, blacks, other non-whites and homosexual individuals, as well as rights for those with disabilities. I also am hopeful because we are the first generations with a serious concern for these rights and the ability to do something about it worldwide.

4. The fourth hopeful sign is the European Union. It represents a hopeful sign even with the French and Dutch rejections of the proposed Constitution. I see those rejections as politically motivated and only temporary. We shall see. Over the last fifty years, the countries of Europe have organized themselves into a new and larger entity that joins the United States, China and India as "major powers" on the world stage. Starting with a few countries joining together after World War II to deal with coal and steel issues, the European Union has grown to encompass most of Europe and already has taken over major functions for 25 European countries. The thirteen American colonies, therefore, are not the only example in the world of "states" joining together and granting some of their "sovereignty" to a new central government for their mutual economic advantage and security.

5. Although unreported and underreported in the media, I am encouraged by the massive pro-civil rights and anti-Vietnam war marches and protests that took place in the United States during the 1960s and 1970s. United States citizens can be moved by key issues! Perhaps they can be moved again by our urgent problems and the need for world government!

6. The protesters at G7 or G8 meetings in Bonn (1985), Berlin (1988-with 80,000 protesters), Genoa (2001-with 300,000 protesters), Ottawa and Halifax (2002), and the protest meetings in Seattle and Atlanta all give me hope. The PEOPLE want to be heard, and the vast majority have been peaceful in their protests! There have been unreported or underreported mass demonstrations around the world for years protesting against GATT, NAFTA, the World Bank and the IMF for ignoring world-wide labor standards and environmental

controls. In one of her columns Molly Ivins takes "the media" to task for ignoring these events or distorting their reports. (28)

7. I am hopeful because of public actions that took place in several countries during spring 2003 when it was clear President George W. Bush intended to proceed with a "preemptive war" against Iraq. The hopeful sign is that in Great Britain, Spain, Indonesia, the United States and other countries massive demonstrations involving millions of people took place to oppose such an invasion. But the biggest surprise was that these demonstrations took place even though the "democratic" governments of these countries were supporting the invasion! Obviously, "the people" were demonstrating against their own governments that were not representing their interests.

8. I am hopeful because of conclaves like the "Second Parliament of World Religions" that took place in Chicago in 1993, in Capetown, South Africa in 1999, and Barcelona, Spain in 2004. The efforts of religious leaders to seek values common to their religions and discuss issues of social concern are a positive move toward finding "common ground" and a more peaceful world.

9. I am hopeful because of the "Microcredit Revolution" that for years has provided opportunities—mostly for women—to take out small, low interest loans to start small businesses in their TLA countries. The "Grameen Bank", "Accion", "Oikocredit" and similar organizations have been very successful in providing opportunities to common folk in TLA countries and even in the United States to break out of their vicious circles of poverty.

10. I am hopeful for the work of Citizens for Global Solutions, a new organization that in 2004 combined the World Federalist Association and the Campaign for UN Reform. The new organization will have a broader reach in seeking a world with peace and justice than either of the organizations that joined to form it could have alone. The new organization seeks world peace and law by whatever means might work, reform of the UN or a new Federal World Government.

11. I am hopeful that most United States citizens in poll after poll express continuing support for the UN despite our government's lack of support for a stronger and more effective UN. We should be more careful in choosing our governmental leaders, and we should vote for those who will support a humane foreign policy and a Limited World Government.

12. I am hopeful because the International Criminal Court is up and running, despite the opposition of the Bush administration.

13. I am hopeful because of the thousands who come each November to Fort Benning, Georgia, to protest at the "Western Hemisphere Institute for Cooperation' (formerly the "School of the Americas"). Over the years military personnel from Latin American countries (including members of "death squads") have learned techniques at this Pentagon-operated facility that have been used to oppress their own people.

14. I am hopeful because <Moveon.org>, <Editor@tompaine.com>, <Alternetheadlines@topica.email-producer.com>, Howard Dean, and others have shown us how to use the Internet to shake the people from political apathy and raise large sums of money in small amounts from citizens for political action.

15. I am hopeful because the 101 recommendations of the blue ribbon UN panel are being taken seriously. Although they do not address critical issues, such as the "veto", the weakness of the General Assembly, the needs for a direct funding source for the UN and a standing UN volunteer Global Peace Force, the 101 recommendations, if implemented, will make the UN more efficient.

16. I am encouraged by the outpouring of concern and billions of dollars of assistance from the world's people and governments following our 9/11 (2001) terrorist attacks and, more recently (December 2004) following the massive South Asia tsunami tragedy. The world's people sense their interconnectedness and responsibility toward each other in ways that surpass most of our governments.

17. I am hopeful because of individuals like Marla Ruzicka, from California, who spent her young life helping others and was killed in Baghdad in April 2005 even as she was trying to help Iraqis whose lives had been disrupted by American military action.

18. I am encouraged that since the 1970s a number of universities have offered courses to help students understand the drives that support militarization and war and the conflict resolution alternatives that are available. Some who have developed such courses are Howard Zinn, Coleman McCarthy and Ronald Glossop. I participated in such a course in the 1980s.

19. And finally, I am hopeful because of statements made by many generals and other leaders through the years relating to the futility of war and the need for some kind of global law and world government. Here are a few more from the Internet:

Pope John XXIII said, speaking of the 1948 Declaration of Human Rights, "The document represents an important step on the path towards the juridicial-political organization of the world community."

David Ben-Gurion, former Prime Minister of Israel, said, "It is a world cooperative commonwealth at which we ought to aim, built on freedom."

President Dwight Eisenhower said in 1960, "Opposed to the idea of two hostile, embittered worlds in perpetual conflict, we envisage a single world community as yet unrealized but advancing rapidly."

Former Communist Party Secretary of the Soviet Union, Mikhail Gorbachev, said in a speech to the UN in December 1988, "Our ideal is a world community of states which are based on the rule of law and which subordinate their foreign policy activities to law."

Too much is at stake for us to go along in old ruts that take us in the wrong direction and let the world come down heavily on our children and grandchildren. We have an urgent need and opportunity to take a different road and move on to a better day for all of the Earth's family. That day can come only through a Limited World Government. We must work together and start now before problems get even more difficult and costly to solve. Keeping in mind these nineteen encouraging signs, we can move ahead with hope.

PART IV

URGENCY AND CHALLENGE

> "Political thinkers are beginning to say, and almost to say with one voice, that the cause of civilization is lost unless national states will agree to abandon some part of their sovereignty."(1)   Lionel Curtis

And Jan Tinburgen said very simply and directly, "Mankind's problems can no longer be solved by national governments. What is needed is world government." (2)

In the 65 years since Curtis wrote those prophetic words "sovereignty" has been slipping away as nations have become more interdependent, even though politicians don't acknowledge it! Our way of life has become so much more violent that the word "civilization" hardly seems appropriate. In those intervening years many other individuals, like Jan Tinburgen in a World Bank report, have echoed Curtis' concerns, but we are still muddling along.

Leonard Pitts in a December 29, 2004 column explained at least part of the cause of the continuing violence and "muddling along" during these decades. He noted that the earlier general acceptance of black inferiority in Southern United States was a case of "if everybody's wrong, (then) nobody's wrong, a communal mindset which allowed white people to commit a social evil, yet still regard themselves as decent." (3)

Pitts' explanation of black slavery and the decades of rampant racism that kept blacks from fulfilling their rights could be applied today to the way we accept the military as useful in providing security, when it can't, and in our uninformed beliefs about others on this planet.

Reves noted in <u>The Anatomy of Peace</u>:

> "to put it bluntly, the meaning of the crisis of the twentieth century (*and our twenty first century as well*) is that this planet must to some degree be brought under unified control. Our task, our duty, is to attempt to institute this unified control (*Limited World Government*) in a democratic way by first proclaiming its principles, and to achieve it by persuasion and with the least possible bloodshed." (4) (Words in *italics* are mine. D.E.C.)

The opportunity for gaining these advantages through Limited World Government will not be open to us indefinitely. Given the world's distress with the United States' preemptive Iraq quagmire and other increasing problems on the one hand and the "hopeful signs" on the other, the window of opportunity to work for a Limited World Government may be open for only a few years.

With all respect due those who over many years have called for "an end to war" and for some kind of world government, many quoted in this book, many of those calls came before urgency and technology have made fulfillment of such pleas possible. I hope my analysis of the urgencies that confront us (Parts I and II), my suggestions for elements needed for a successful world government and my explanation of three alternative approaches to setting up a world government (Part III) will not be a hollow call, but a call to action!

People are not puppets. We are not sheep. But we in the United States have been lulled to sleep for years by manipulated "news" that repeats the self-serving spin of governments and corporations. We also have been driven in our consumerism by relentless advertising and obsolescence built into our purchases. For years we have been fed a diet of how great are our individual freedoms with little to help us understand our equally important responsibilities to each other and to our communities. Is this brainwashing? Probably. We know brainwashing can happen, but we also know that brainwashing can be reversed by repeated doses of the truth.

We are reasonably intelligent people who want to live in peace and we want our governments to help us…or, in President Eisenhower's words, "Get out of the way" so we can organize an effective world government!

Stephen Mallaby went even further in his March-April 2002 <u>Foreign Affairs</u> article:

> "The chaos of the world is too threatening to ignore and existing methods for dealing with that chaos *(the military approach)* have been tried and found wanting." He also said America and her allies "must either mold the international machinery to address the problems of their times….or they can muddle along until some future collection of leaders rises to the challenge." (5) (Words in *italics* are mine. D.E.C.)

The human family can't wait until some undetermined time in the future when more "clear-headed leaders" might appear. NOW is the critical time if we are really concerned about the kind of future we will be leaving for our children and those who follow! People around the world need to convince their governments NOW to support efforts toward world government. As explained in Part III, if governments are not interested, "the people" must do it themselves! And they CAN!

A. A WEB OF SURVIVAL

In Part I our "Troubled World of Extremes" was discussed. A point emphasized was the interrelatedness of everything that goes on in a "place", including intermingled aspects of natural environments and cultural characteristics and diverse people. It was shown how it is impossible to solve a single problem without involving many aspects of life in that "place".

In Part II key problems (war and militarization, corporate globalization, our energy problem, deteriorating environment and population growth) were examined in relation to other problems and aspects of our cultural and natural environments. None of these can be solved in isolation. All require a global approach to their solution.

To visualize these interrelationships we might imagine an American Indian dream catcher with many threads crossing a circle (Figure 2). Each thread crosses others, leaving a small opening in the center. The legend of the dream catcher is that, if a dream catcher is placed over a person as he or she sleeps, the bad dreams will be caught up in the web and good dreams will slip through the center opening to give that person a peaceful sleep.

Using the dream catcher model, points 1, 2 and 3 at the top of the circle represent the three key problems the human family faces in this writer's judgment. Points around the rest of Figure 2's circle represent avenues of solution to these three key problems. Lines crossing the circle and connecting these points represent those web-like interrelationships. Threads from each point on the circle touch as they pass the center opening. The center opening itself, point 16, represents HOPE and PRIDE.

Because all lines touch the center, HOPE and PRIDE can be considered important "keys" to the accomplishment of the solution strategies around the circle. Every person needs HOPE and PRIDE in whatever they do, although many of our fellow citizens on this planet do not have much of either. Hope energizes us to accomplish our dreams. It inspires and, like a magnet, draws people

A WEB OF SURVIVAL

At the top of the Circle are Three Key Problems Facing Mankind. Below these problems are suggestions for overcoming each. Around the rest of the Circle are suggested actions that also need to be taken: items 4 - 7 by the world community and items 8 - 10 by the United States. Items 11 - 15 MUST be part of a modified UN or a Limited World Government (LWG). To overcome Problems 1 - 3 and accomplish items 4 - 15, we ALL need HOPE and PRIDE, item 16.

THE THREE KEY PROBLEMS

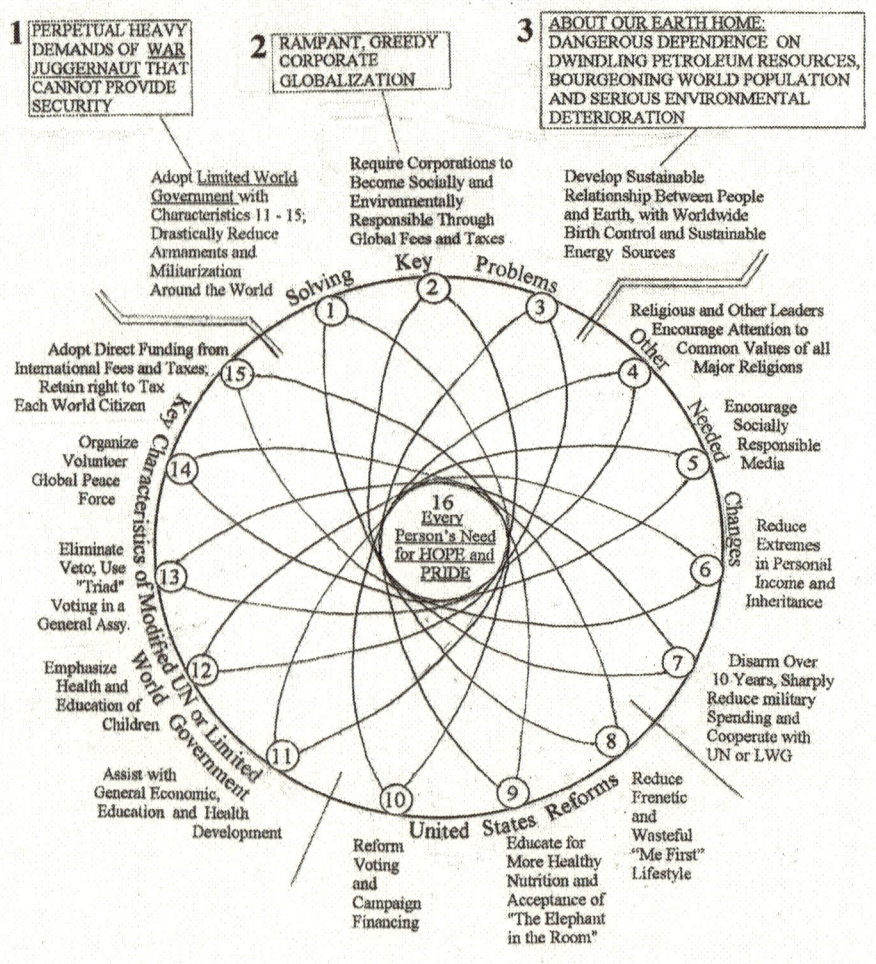

1 PERPETUAL HEAVY DEMANDS OF WAR JUGGERNAUT THAT CANNOT PROVIDE SECURITY

2 RAMPANT, GREEDY CORPORATE GLOBALIZATION

3 ABOUT OUR EARTH HOME: DANGEROUS DEPENDENCE ON DWINDLING PETROLEUM RESOURCES, BOURGEONING WORLD POPULATION AND SERIOUS ENVIRONMENTAL DETERIORATION

Adopt Limited World Government with Characteristics 11 - 15; Drastically Reduce Armaments and Militarization Around the World

Require Corporations to Become Socially and Environmentally Responsible Through Global Fees and Taxes

Develop Sustainable Relationship Between People and Earth, with Worldwide Birth Control and Sustainable Energy Sources

Adopt Direct Funding from International Fees and Taxes; Retain right to Tax Each World Citizen

Religious and Other Leaders Encourage Attention to Common Values of all Major Religions

Organize Volunteer Global Peace Force

Encourage Socially Responsible Media

Eliminate Veto; Use "Triad" Voting in a General Assy.

16 Every Person's Need for HOPE and PRIDE

Reduce Extremes in Personal Income and Inheritance

Emphasize Health and Education of Children

Disarm Over 10 Years, Sharply Reduce military Spending and Cooperate with UN or LWG

Assist with General Economic, Education and Health Development

Reduce Frenetic and Wasteful "Me First" Lifestyle

Reform Voting and Campaign Financing

Educate for More Healthy Nutrition and Acceptance of "The Elephant in the Room"

Solving Key Problems
Other Needed Changes
Key Characteristics of Modified UN or Limited World Government
United States Reforms

D.E.C. - 2004

Figure 2

together to work for a better tomorrow. Hope is the engine of the future. And Pride helps each of us to stand tall with satisfaction over jobs well done, especially jobs that help others and make things better for our children and those who will follow.

Arundhati Roy and others have said that every person, every citizen of the world, has a right to food, water, shelter, and dignity. Having HOPE and PRIDE can go a long way toward fulfilling each person's need to live his or her life with DIGNITY!

B. WHAT CAN WE DO?

This is a crucial question for those who are convinced that a Limited World Government is necessary and possible. A reaction from many might be that they already are too busy to take on a new project. To that argument the question should be: "Which is more important, your TV program?....playing or watching games?....OR taking action to help bring about the kind of world you really want to leave for your children?"

If you are not convinced of the need for a Limited World Government by what I have written or by the quotes that are included, perhaps you are moved by one of the other important issues discussed in this book. Your concern may be about the wastefulness of militarization that can bring no security. Or perhaps you are concerned about the perils of corporate globalization, or the need for a long-term sustainable relationship between the Earth's human family and our Earth home. Perhaps you want to do something about the critical need for alternative energy sources or the coming fresh water crunch or the growing gap between rich and poor everywhere in the world. If you are moved by any of these take action! Warriors are needed in the trenches on all of these issues.

In his <u>A Democratic Manifesto</u> Reves tells us:

> "Democracy is not and never can be a closed, rigid system. This is its death. Any closed rigid system must lead to wars, revolutions and dictatorships. Democracy needs constant readjustment. Its institutions require ceaseless rejuvenation....Democracy is an atmosphere, the only atmosphere in which modern man can live, prosper and progress.
> "The political organization which is required to solve the problems of war and peace, of freedom and slavery (*Limited World Government*), is not a distant, remote aim, but an immediate necessity." (6) (Words in *italics* are mine. D.E.C.)

In recent years the media, too interested in the "bottom line", has not done a good job to help create an "informed electorate". Almost gone are the investigative reporters of yesteryear who probed issues to find truth "for the people". Schools have become preoccupied with their students' success in passing government prescribed minimum level tests. In this "Me First" time in our country's history, schools have pandered to "patriotism" but have not helped much in preparing students to strengthen their communities or understand the fragility of our democracy. Too many of all ages have become mesmerized by TV entertainment.

In the past, attending a play, a concert, a vaudeville performance or ball game was a once-in-a-while special event for most people and "family games" at home were common. Now one has access to hundreds of mind-bending and mind-dulling entertainment options 24/7 at home with the touch of a finger on a TV "remote". Families and neighbors socializing together has declined sharply.

There are many ways individuals can help with solutions to the war problem and other critical problems discussed in this book. In addition to the suggestions that follow, both Paul Simon and Emery Reves include suggestions how individuals can take action to further the concerns they raised in the conclusions of their books. Their suggestions also are relevant here.

I hope the suggestions that follow will be of particular interest to young people and to educators. After all, preparing the public to think about world government intelligently represents a challenging job. One must overcome longstanding concepts about the history of one's country and nationalism and sovereignty that are not helpful in facing the realities of a world of interdependent people and nations. Two books come to mind that can help develop a more "people oriented" view of United States history. These are: A People's History of the United States by Howard Zinn (ISBN 0-06-192643-0), and Lies My Teacher Told Me by James W. Loewen (ISBN 0-684-81886-8).

The FIRST step is to become informed about the critical issues and their possible solutions. Learning something about the history of these issues also is helpful. Don't be intimidated by feelings of inadequacy or being one of a small minority that sees the critical importance of a particular issue or the need for a Limited World Government. Throughout history all movements for important changes start with a small group of informed and active individuals.

On the Internet you can find something on virtually any current or historic topic, and topics like world government, United Nations, and globalization will yield provide important information.

The following also provide insights into current news: TrueMajority.org., indypress.org, altpress.org, and Commondreams.org. Some others already have been mentioned. These present information and encourage action on many problems that involve people and our government (See Appendix G). On the Internet look up Garry Davis, who disavowed his American citizenship after World War II and declared himself "the world's first world citizen". He remains active and has published two books and other materials about world government and world citizenship.

Once you have gathered information and confidence concerning the issue of your choice or the need for world government, a SECOND way individuals can help push for needed changes is to talk with those who have similar interests to share sources and ideas. Then you can write "Letters to the Editor" of your local newspaper to share your knowledge and feelings to stimulate the interest of readers in your community. Letters can be written as questions to leaders or as analysis of data about an issue. As a "lead in" statement for such letters include one or two statements of fact about the issue. Letters need not be specifically about world government to help educate the public on world issues. Editors do prefer that letters relate somehow to their city or area, but virtually everything has a relationship with one of the key issues noted in this book or to a more peaceful world! Letters published will help educate the public and bring out individuals who also may write letters and become active in the endeavor.

What is there to write about in such letters? Here are a few suggestions that touch on local and national "people" issues that relate to war and how governments should work for the people and would also generate public interest. Many of these items do not touch directly on the UN or world government, but they can focus on an issue and how our government works in relation to people needs and to the rest of the world.

1. Taxes should not be reduced and the Estate Tax should not be eliminated for estates valued over a few million dollars. Why? With our massive and increasing national debt and deficit we should not be reducing taxes! Revenue generated by taxes was collected to do many necessary things "for the people", and our schools, hospitals, roads, bridges all need major investment. Revenue could help fund a new GI Bill for returning Iraq War veterans

or pay for educational improvements across our country and the world. Our tax dollars also could fund intensive research on alternative energy sources or how to face up to global warming.

2. Taxes should not be reduced because we must reduce our enormous national debt. By using part of tax revenue to reduce the national debt we will save the billions of dollars we pay each year as interest on that debt. The United States pays almost as much interest on its debt each year as it does to the Pentagon! Banks and other financial institutions make their profits from lending money to individuals and governments. But responsible borrowers pay off their debts. And so should the United States government! We do not need to subsidize our banks and financial institutions! Another reason taxes should not be reduced is because of the Iraq war, which is costing us over a billion dollars a week and is not over.

3. Regardless how unwise that war is, we are in it. We could declare "victory" and pull out, as we did in Vietnam, leaving the Iraqi people in chaos with little hope of their following through and becoming a democracy. Another way to change the dynamics of the war is for the United States to turn the Iraq mess over to the United Nations. We should shift to the sidelines and provide help requested by the UN to rebuild what we destroyed and help Iraq toward democracy.

4. The November 2000 and 2004 elections in the United States revealed serious flaws in our voting procedures and equipment and in our electoral process. Preserving our democracy through voting and campaign finance reforms should be of importance to all citizens. Imagine our reaction to a foreign election in Great Britain or Italy or India that was finally decided by a Supreme Court. Perhaps the only positive thing that can be said about those two national elections in the United States is that, compared to contested elections in other countries, transitions were made peacefully and neither led to bloodshed or fighting in the streets.

5. Citizens need to learn about the interdependence of all nations on many critical materials and how international trade makes possible the high tech way of life in TA countries. Citizens also need to learn about the poverty and difficult living conditions where most people of the world live. International trade and interdependence also nullify the "sovereignty" that nations treasured in earlier times.

6. People everywhere need to learn the truth about the dwindling supply of crude oil in the world and encourage efficient use of that one-time-use

resource. We must purchase more efficient automobiles, and use of public transport. Intensive research on alternative energy sources, including oil shale, should be encouraged by governments and universities, with the government or the university retaining rights to new processes developed.

A THIRD way to "do something" is to actually join one or more of the national organizations that deal with international or global or world government issues, and pay their modest dues (<u>Appendix G1</u>). Look up and join organizations like Citizens for Global Solutions (the new organization combining the World Federalist Association and the Campaign for UN Reform). The United Nations Association of the USA (UNA-USA) is another organization whose members favor and work for reform of the UN to make it more effective. The "Philadelphia II" organization seeks to amend our Constitution to lead us toward participation in a world government.

Many organizations have newsletters and local organizations. People interested in Limited World Government are encouraged to become active in one or more organizations to develop support and pursue solutions to the global problems from a local base. Furthermore, there always is strength and encouragement being a member of a group focused on an issue. Individuals are encouraged to form local chapters of these organizations.

And a FOURTH way: Become involved in the political process itself! Political parties themselves can also be included as places to become active to support issues of concern to you. Attend public meetings that relate to world issues, and especially meetings where candidates for state and national public offices are presenting their points of view. Don't hesitate to engage candidates with hard questions about their positions on the UN, the ICC, the military budget, foreign aid, world government, international (global) law, and other world related topics.

And a last point: Consider becoming a candidate yourself or encourage and support world-minded individuals to run for office. Reflecting on the Jimmy Stewart movie classic, "Mr. Smith Goes to Washington", we need more "Mr. Smiths" in Washington!

Each individual will decide the best way to follow through and become active. This decision also will depend on the person's interest and what is available in his or her community. Whatever we do, we must not be discouraged by small numbers of individuals working for world government. Despite the urgency, important things usually do not happen fast.

As further things that might be done, religious leaders around the world must deemphasize their competition and their differences with other religions. Instead they must emphasize the commonalities of their religious teachings with other religions. Emphasizing the Golden Rule and the last five or six of the Ten Commandments might be a good place to start. The world's people, regardless of their cultural history and religious beliefs emphasized in the past, must learn these commonalities and embrace them and live by them if we are ultimately to have a world community in which all people, even with their differences, will be comfortable with each other.

A similar case must be made for educational efforts and systems around the world, and the media. Ultimately the development and success of a Limited World Government must depend on an education process that is furthered by all elements of the media in schools, in homes, and everywhere people meet. Teaching and learning must help students at all levels (including adults!) to understand how all people in all countries are interdependent, how we all have similar aspirations, and how urgent it is that we work together to solve the critical challenges facing all of us. We must learn that most people in the world, regardless of how rich or poor, want to live in peace.

We must not let ourselves be distracted and "entertained" like the people of ancient Rome with bloody games in the Coliseum—or on TV! We must set aside our "spectatoritis", our fixation with sitcoms and games on TV or playing computer games. We *must* get involved and work together if we are to find long term answers that can bring peace, security and a reasonable prosperity to everyone.

Perhaps the people of the world can learn from the motto and symbol of Tongji University in Shanghai, which Carol and I visited in 1989. The stylized symbol of the University shows three people poling a boat. The University's motto, so relevant to our common humanity on this fragile yet enduring planet is: "People in the same boat must work together." So true!

C. THE ATHENIANS

Edward Gibbon wrote about the ancient Athenians,

> "In the end more than they (Athenians in ancient Greece) wanted freedom, they wanted security. They wanted a comfortable life, and they lost it all—security, comfort, and freedom. When the Athenians finally wanted not to give to society but for society to give to them, when the freedom they wished for was freedom from responsibility, then Athens ceased to be free and was never free again." (7)

That is what is happening in the United States as I write. Our democracy is being compromised in an impossible search for "security". When we focus only on terrorists or Iraq, we are not going after the basic enemy. Individuals in our government are distracting us from the real enemies. The real enemies we must attack are those problems that will undermine our way of life if left unattended. We must rid ourselves of arrogance and greed. We must abandon any thoughts of dominating the world. We must rid ourselves of our apathy toward our nation's and the world's problems. Terrorism is only a symptom of deeper problems.

War and militarization, arrogance in governing, global warming, depletion of liquid petroleum, the increasing demands for fresh water in the world, greedy corporations, our burgeoning world population, the "me first" attitude and lifestyle of so many individuals, and the need for a sustainable balance between humans and our Earth home...These are the real issues that we must engage before it is too late! Perhaps we induced the Soviet Union into bankruptcy through the arms race, but we are on the way to doing it to ourselves through our Iraq quagmire.

To combat these, all passengers on "Spaceship Earth" must cooperate with other passengers and we must develop the social machinery that can handle these critical issues. Thus in every democratic country we must vote into office those individuals who will deal seriously with problems within each country, but also candidates who also will help us cooperate sincerely with the rest of the world. We must join and work with organizations that are pursuing global goals "for the people". If we want peace we must work to help the world's people.

We must adopt a Limited World Government so globalization can be controlled. At a June 2004 meeting of the UN Conference on Trade and Development, Brazil's new president, Luiz Inacio Lula da Silva, said that:

> "Instead of benefiting multinational corporations, globalization should be harnessed to help poor countries gain greater market access, higher living standards and more funding to improve infrastructure and technology." (8)

The vast majority of United States citizens pay their income taxes on time. I am one of them, but I bight my tongue each year as I pay because I know about half of what I pay goes down the black hole of the military approach that can not provide real long-term security anywhere. Living behind a wall of big guns is not security and does not represent a true "civilization" as most of us conceive it.

Iraq is showing us you can't force democracy on a people at the end of a gun. We also should know that by now regardless of old Western movies and Florida's new gun-carrying law. Security can come only with reasonable and enforced laws. Because of this disconnect the government misrepresents what it is doing. The odds of finding long-term security by the military are less than winning in the lotteries state governments have adopted as an unfair method of balancing their budgets!

The world does not have the time or the money for war! We should not waste our treasure and the lives of our young service men and women on wars over dwindling supplies of petroleum that will become too costly in only a few decades. Instead of spending on the military, we should subsidize scientists to find energy substitutes, and modify our lifestyle and our cities to use less energy. We should help scientists focus on research to deal with global warming and develop ways to deal with it as soon and as best we can.

The interrelatedness of everything and all we do on Earth is demonstrated again by a quote in Peter Singer's <u>One World</u>. Here he is quoting from a UN report:

"In the global village, someone else's poverty very soon becomes one's own problem: lack of markets for one's products, illegal immigration, pollution, contagious disease, insecurity, fanaticism, terrorism." (9)

Notice especially the last three words of that Singer quote.

Singer suggests that everyone with an income "greater than enough" to provide reasonable necessities for oneself and family should give 1% of their income to those in need of food, clean water, shelter and health care. As modest as Singer's proposal sounds it *would* be a significant as well as a symbolic start toward helping others on our planet that could quell the fires of terrorism. Perhaps a 1% tax on better-off people could be the basis of a world wide tax to support a Limited World Government and its programs to aid those in poverty. Singer also says that doing this should not be seen as a heroic act, but to fail to do so would show indifference to the human family (10).

As Paul Simon also said on this point:

"Would we all be richer if we fairly dramatically reduced poverty within our nation and around the world? To ask the question is to answer it. Reducing poverty will require a temporary small sacrifice on the part of many of us (*the elephant in the room?*)—with big pay-offs in the long run—but the big barrier is not the dollars but the will, which comes from the belief that real change can be effected." (11) (Words in *italics* are mine. D.E.C.)

Think of what could be gained by our "rejoining the world" and attacking poverty at home and abroad. Paul Simon reminds us of Martin Luther King, Junior's powerful quote, "Those who make peaceful revolution impossible will make violent revolutions inevitable." (12) Paul also reminds us of what President Truman said, "The responsibility of a great state is to serve and not to dominate the world." (13)

For starters, the United States over a few years could reduce its military budget and inventory by half, and then more, and we would still have by far the largest military establishment in the world! As has been pointed out, the billions of dollars saved and the scientific talent available (released from the military) could address other problems pressing on humans everywhere, and the United States would regain some of the positive image it has lost in recent years.

In his 1992 book, "Earth in the Balance", then Senator Al Gore devoted an entire chapter to his proposal for a "Global Marshall Plan", a massive plan similar to the plan by which the United States helped rebuild Western Europe after World

War II. (14) Think about the possibilities of a global development plan managed by a Limited World Government, paid for by savings from reduced military expenditures! Consider how the United States could regain a respected place among the nations of the world by participating in such a venture!

Here again is this very unbalanced "either-or" choice: We can join efforts toward a Limited World Government and gain the long-term benefits of "peace with law", OR stumble along with things as they are and, with the rest of the world, suffer the consequences of even more violence, terrorism, devastating wars, and probable loss of our democracy in the decades ahead.

The problems pressing on our door will not go away and will bring the Western world to its knees if they are not dealt with soon. Much of the TLA world is already on its knees, so they have less to lose from inaction. In any case, the TA world, the "Western world", has the power and control; the TLA world has neither. Action is up to the Western world, especially the United States. What greater security can we in the Western world provide for our future and for our children than to deal with those issues now? And a Limited World Government is the only way we can deal with these global issues.

Several times before in human history major changes in technology have reverberated throughout the world and all cultures. In the last two centuries alone massive changes have been brought on by inventions like the steam engine, the automobile, airplane, TV and computer. Each revolutionized our lives in different ways.

The computer, Internet and international air travel are supporting corporate globalization, but they also are revolutionizing international discourse and, with other technological advances, they *are* helping us toward some kind of world community. But is corporate globalization the kind of world community we want?

In times past, as we shifted from one chapter in the human saga to another, workers tending horses and those making bows and arrows, armor, wagons, buggy whips, wooden sailboats and barrels and many other items had to find new jobs. A world at peace would open great opportunities for new technologies and worldwide markets, but there would be major dislocations during transition years. Earlier major shifts took generations, even centuries, to spread around the world. Our shift toward a global community must be telescoped into only a few decades!

What else do we know? If people have the basics of life and jobs and dignity in their work, they very likely will NOT be terrorists. Crime rates decline sharply when individuals get a job with an adequate and dependable income!

The United States is the most powerful nation the world has ever known in so many ways. We can help lead the world to a Limited World Government and a better day for all. Or, if we do not, we will suffer with the rest of the world when our way of life—along with much in the rest of the world—will decline in not too many years. How we respond to the choice before us should not be a difficult if we keep our children and grandchildren in mind!

D. CONCLUSION

Will the human family rise to the many challenges in time to avert major upheavals around the world? Even if we start down the road to form a world government soon is it too late to overcome the inertia of the status quo?

Can we bring population growth in the world to a halt? Can we take giant steps in developing alternative energy sources? Can we bridle the war monster? Can we rein in multinational corporations that know no loyalty to persons, communities or nations?

And of course to all of these questions there can be no "for sure" answers. We need strong forward-looking leaders to help us, but as thinking, rational creatures concerned for our children and those who will follow, if leaders will not do it "we the people" must work together to do it ourselves. That is the only way each of us can reach the end of our days with a clear conscience of having tried to help a worthy cause during our years.

The terrorist attacks have brought on changes in most countries in airports and ports and government agencies. The terrorists also have given us a challenge and opened an opportunity for everyone to rethink and act on the big, long-term questions of fairness and justice in the world and the need for a reformed United Nations or a Limited World Government.

Some still might say, "Don't bother with those issues. Go after the terrorists!" To which I repeat that terrorism is only a symptom of problems in the world. In my judgment it is far more than a coincidence that the tragedy of 9/11 has not been repeated in the United States. Some will say, "But homeland security has prevented another attack!" Maybe so. But consider how easy a repeat would be, given our many open land borders, our long coastlines, our vulnerable ports, power plants and factories, and the ease with which small packages of powerful explosives could be brought in. Terrorists do not need to hijack airplanes or use intercontinental missiles to disrupt and demoralize us! If terrorists really wanted to destroy our way of life, they could have disrupted us over and over in so many critical and deadly ways in these last four years IF that was what "9/11" was all about. But I do not believe that was their intent or their message.

No doubt some terrorists do object to the free-wheeling, flamboyant lifestyle of some "Americans". However, I believe the basic terrorist message from the start has been a message to the United States about the inconsistency and lack of morality in our foreign policy over many decades, our arrogance, our domination and stinginess with the UN, our niggardliness in foreign aid, the imbalance in our dealings with Israel and the Palestinians, our greedy corporations, and most recently—our preemptive invasion and occupation of Iraq. I am confident the terrorists and most people around the world know more about and remember more clearly than most United States citizens our CIA and White House involvements over many decades in illegalities, assassinations, and supporting dictators rather than movements of the people for a better life.

I believe terrorists are trying to tell us—and any friends we may still have around the world—about of all of these things. In my judgment this is not a general confrontation between Christianity and Islam, although there are fanatic extremists who identify with both religions. I believe the terrorists do not want to bring our country to its knees because they too know what a power for good our country can be if it lives up to its ideals. I believe they simply want us to use our power and ingenuity to help the world and not to dominate!

Make no mistake in interpreting the above paragraphs. I do not condone or support terrorism. All terrorist acts are despicable. Those who commit murder and mayhem against others under any guise should be apprehended and dealt with under the law. My plea is that we also look behind terrorist acts and deal with possible reasons for such extremist acts.

Further, I respect and support our troops who have volunteered to serve the United States and follow the orders of their commanders. I sincerely believe they were misled as to their mission which has become a mission impossible. As distasteful as it might be to our leaders, and as was suggested, we should turn the Iraq quagmire over to the UN and work with and support that organization to find and implement reasonable solutions.

Introducing his 2004 book, The Choice, Zgigniew Brzezinski wrote:

> "America, therefore, confronts a unique paradox: it is the first and only global superpower…(It is) preoccupied with threats from a variety of much weaker hostile sources….

"The quest for a wise foreign policy must begin with the realization that 'globalization' in its essence means global interdependence....

"Ultimately, the central policy question confronting America is 'Hegemony *(leadership, dominance)* for the sake of what?'" (15) (Words in *italics* are mine. D.E.C.)

It is inhumane and immoral to let the exploitations and deprivations of most of our fellow passengers on this planet continue in support of the "Western" way of life. And why is that so now more than in times past? Because until our generations, all thoughts about "world community" and "eliminating war" and "world government" were idle dreams or mere hopes. We know now it is a necessity and can become reality.

WE ARE THE FIRST GENERATIONS IN HUMAN HISTORY WITH COMMUNICATION AND TECHNOLOGICAL CAPABILITY TO ACTUALLY REALIZE A TRUE WORLD WIDE CIVILIZATION, IN ALL THAT SHOULD MEAN. WE ARE THE FIRST GENERATIONS WITH A SHARPENED CONCERN FOR HUMAN RIGHTS AND THE ABILITY TO MAKE HUMAN RIGHTS REAL FOR THE ENTIRE HUMAN FAMILY!

It won't be easy, but it can be done if we have the will and the heart to do it! But again on the other hand, what are the choices? Either, as rational human beings, we make intelligent choices for our children's and grandchildren's future, or their future will be bleak.

The strongest basis for hope in this urgent either-or scenario is that in any true democracy the PEOPLE HAVE THE POWER TO MAKE CHOICES! As intelligent, reasoning human beings, United States citizens and others who live in reasonable democracies still have the opportunity and the obligation to make choices and changes in our governments and their policies that can have positive worldwide repercussions.

Along this same line, there still is ample time for President George W. Bush to dismiss his neo-conservative advisors and adopt a foreign policy that is people friendly and world embracing. His popularity would rise from the depths and he would go down in history as a great leader, not as just another leader focusing on the short term who tried to dominate the world.

As was quoted earlier, Victor Hugo said, "Nothing else in the world...not all the armies...is so powerful as an idea whose time has come." An "enlightened globalization" and "world community" and "Limited World Government" are such ideas! They MUST be realized soon or the human experiment on Earth may falter for many decades.

In the Introduction to his <u>Healing America</u>, Paul Simon said,

> "If the world's most powerful nation renews these values (humility, compassion, equality of opportunity, participation, integrity and respect) and has a vision of what we can do to build a better society and a better world, our country will be an immeasurably greater constructive force. My hope is that people in our country will benefit from this examination, and that at least a few other countries might become more aware of our striving for goodness and good will. We can learn from our history; we can learn from each other. And others will see our hopes for the best in us by our good example." (16)

And near the end of his book Paul Simon said,

> "There is a growing sense that humanity is not divisible; that while we are proud to be Americans, we have a common bond with all people; that in addition to being loyal American citizens, we also should be loyal world citizens. To the extent such sensitivity is nurtured, it is less likely that our children will be involved in violent conflicts or become victims of terrorist attacks." (17)

So it may well be up to us in the United States to take the lead in instituting a Limited World Government. And we the people have the power through thousands of voting booths and public meetings and the Internet and letters to the editor to let our wishes and candidate choices be known.

In ending this book I repeat two quotes that I included in the Introduction. Remember the Mayor of Hiroshima's quote? It is the next to last quote in the booklet, "Can America Learn About Peace and Freedom From…":

> "It is not my place to tell Americans what ought to be done. But what I can do is to tell them about what will happen to the world's cities if something is not done to stop war….We know that stopping war is not a simple thing….We know, too, that peace is not to be had just for the asking: all nations must agree to it.
> "But we also know that some nation must take leadership. America can call for world law, and all the world will listen….Let the call go out from America for a federation of the nations strong enough to

prevent war, and a thrill will be known in the hearts of millions of people everywhere." (18)

And the last quote in that 1958 booklet is by Henry L. Stimson (Secretary of State under Herbert Hoover, Secretary of War under F. D. Roosevelt) and also is a challenge to the United States:

> "How soon this nation will fully understand the size and nature of its present mission, I do not dare to say. But I venture to assert that in a very large degree the future of mankind depends on the answer to this question. And I am confident that if the issues are clearly presented, the American people will give the right answer." (19)

I have done my best to present the issues and the alternatives clearly. If enough people study these issues and take it to heart and take hold of this challenge, we can begin to heal our world right away, even as we know that the healing process will take years. Paul Simon concluded his book, <u>Healing America</u>, with these words:

> "It will not take hundreds of thousands of people to cause positive movement. A handful in each congressional district and in each state can reenergize us. I hope you will be among that handful who help to change the course of history for the better....You can help the nation *(and the world)* to heal itself....You can help the nation *(and the world)* dream once again." (20) (Words in *italics* are mine. D.E.C.)

EPILOGUE

Obviously I am concerned about what kind of world will be there for all grandchildren when they take over the world in just a few decades. I do not believe in an Armageddon-type ending to the human experiment on Earth. The Earth will continue spinning around the sun for billions of years. What happens to the Earth's human family for good or ill will be because of what people do—or do not do.

Let me repeat Arthur Schopenhauer's observation about public acceptance of a "truth":

> "All truth passes through three stages. First, it is ridiculed. Second, it is violently opposed. Third, it is accepted as being self-evident." (1)

The testimony of many quoted in this book lends credibility to the "truth" of Limited World Government if the human experiment on Earth is to succeed. It also is likely that Limited World Government will have Schopenhauer's three stage reception: It is being and will be dismissed by many as a dreamy idea that may come some time in the future. Once consideration of the idea "takes hold", as it did for a few years after World War II, and as we move toward establishment of a Limited World Government, it will be opposed by those whose lives will be disrupted.

And then, a decade or two after a Limited World Government has been in place and proved itself with a more prosperous and peaceful world, the concept will be accepted and acknowledged as the self-evident solution to the world's many problems. And the wonderment will be "Why didn't we humans get our act together sooner?" Whether this happens in a decade or two or more it will have become a "self-evident truth!"

The United States, the most powerful nation the world has ever known, must lead the world in drawing down its military and helping establish a Limited World Government. In doing so, we will go down in history as the greatest nation ever. The names of our leaders who led the way will be heroes to all mankind and will be touted in history books forever. And our children and grandchildren—and all children and grandchildren around the world—will thank us for our efforts!

Here are a few more quotes about our desperate need for world law and world government to overcome the cancer of war and other problems that threaten the entire human family:

> "Those of us who are living today can influence the future of civilization. We can influence whether our planet will drift into chaos and violence, or whether through a monumental educational and political effort we will achieve a world of peace under a system of law where individual violators of that law are brought to justice....We need a system of enforceable world law—a democratic world government—to deal with world problems."
>
> Walter Cronkite (2)

> "We are more than ever committed to the rule of law—in our own land and around the world. We believe more than ever in the rights of man, all men of every color—in our own land and around the world. And more than ever we support the United Nations, as the best instrument yet devised to promote the peace of the world and well-being of mankind."
>
> President Lyndon B. Johnson,
> Address to the United Nations,
> December 1963 (3)

> "As I review the march of world events in recent years, I am ever more deeply convinced that the United Nations represents the soundest hope for peace in the world. For this reason I believe that the processes of the United Nations need further to be developed and strengthened.
> "I speak particularly of increasing its (the UN's) ability to secure justice under international law....The peace we seek and need means

much more than mere absence of war. It means the acceptance of law and the fostering of justice in all the world."

President Dwight D. Eisenhower
October 31, 1956 (4)

Where do I see the United States' two major political parties on this endeavor? In my opinion and on virtually every issue raised in this book, I see the Republicans on the wrong track. As for the Democrats, they don't seem to even have a working track at this time.

I refer you again to <u>Appendix B</u>, but especially to <u>Appendix B2</u>. If people of goodwill the world over who are truly religious and caring would live by those 7 precepts, we and those who will follow us would live in a more peaceful world.

* * * * *

So there you have it: This retired geographer sharing his deep and urgent concerns about what we are doing to our Earth home and to ourselves. You also know of my strong belief that the three critical global issues I identify can be dealt with only by global action through a reformed United Nations or a new Limited World Government.

This father and "grandpa" believes other parents and grandparents—and some of my thousands of Southern Illinois University students through thirty-some years—will not want to leave a poisoned, violent and chaotic world as their children's heritage. Perhaps many will be informed and emboldened to take action as Paul Simon—and Sheila—have encouraged us to do.

APPENDICES

APPENDIX A: OUR DIVIDED WORLD

A1. FOUR-FIFTHS OF THE WORLD
(Technologically Less-Advanced Areas/Nations—"TLA")

1. Includes four-fifths of the world's people, over half living in Asia (one-fifth in China; one-sixth in India).

2. Three-fourths of the world's people are brown, tan or black skinned. Most live in TLA areas.

3. Most Latin Americans are Catholic Christians. Elsewhere in the TLA world most are Muslims, Hindus, Buddhist, non-religious and animists.

4. Many are poorly fed. There are significant food losses to rodents, pests, rot, and corruption.

5. Many are sick and need medical care. Medical facilities are very inadequate for most people. Life expectancy is short and AIDS is a serious problem.

6. Except in cities and towns, most are illiterate with limited world knowledge.

7. Most live in small farming villages in rural areas with large families and rapid population growth. Major cities, many with all modern amenities, are growing rapidly with massive "shanty towns".

8. Most families earn livelihood by subsistence farming, mining and crafts. In cities, services and multinational corporations provide some employment.

9. In rural areas most are poor in dollar incomes, but there is an emerging middle class and a wealthy and controlling elite minority.

10. Most people depend little on general trade, but many of their governments depend on one or two agricultural specialties or mineral exports. In recent decades some have been advantaged by "outsourced" manufacturing from TA areas.

11. Many governments are inexperienced or unstable with high levels of corruption, bribery and debt. Human rights are not of primary concern.

12. All are experiencing a ferment of change and a "Revolution of Rising Expectations", with incentives for emigration and terrorism.

13. As they struggle to industrialize, there is little concern for environmental issues or long term consequences.

14. Despite their poverty, many governments spend a large portion of revenue on military equipment, training, and interest paid to TA banks on old loans.

A2. ONE-FIFTH OF THE WORLD
(Technologically Advanced Areas/Nations—"TA")

1. Includes only one-fifth of the world's population. Most live in North America, Europe, Western Russia and Japan.

2. Most are Caucasian with increasing numbers of non-white minorities.

3. Most are Christian (except Japan), with increasing numbers of Muslims, Hindus and Buddhists. Many are non-religious in Russia, Europe and the US.

4. Despite the prevalence of junk foods, most are reasonably fed, although obesity is acknowledged as a problem in the US.

5. Except for non-whites in the US, most are in good health with a long average life span. Many in the US have no health care insurance.

6. Most are literate and have the opportunity to be reasonably informed about the world. In the US most have limited truthful world knowledge.

7. The vast majority live as families and single individuals in towns and cities. Population growth is slow.

8. Most have highly commercialized economies with high development of Research and Development activities. Common use of high tech: automation in manufacturing, computers, cell phones, fax, etc.

9. With many two wage-earner families, incomes are adequate for the needs of most. In the US a large "underclass" exists and a burgeoning wealthy elite.

10. Economies and ways of life are vulnerable, highly interdependent and very dependent on trade, especially in petroleum, some minerals and food.

11. Most governments are mature, experienced and reasonably democratic and corruption-free.

12. There are disquieting clues to dissatisfactions of many with the long term viability of the TA way of life. "Terrorism" is a significant problem.

13. Most have environment movements and some environment protection laws. Virtually all except the US have joined international treaties to address critical global environment issues.

14. Several, especially the US, spend heavily for military purposes and a few sell military materials to TLA nations.

APPENDIX B:
POINTS AGREED UPON BY WORLD RELIGIOUS LEADERS

B1: Seven points agreed upon by religious leaders at 1970 meeting:

1. An acknowledgment of the fundamental unity of the human family, of the equality and dignity of all human beings.

2. A sense of the sacredness of the individual person and his conscience.

3. A sense of the value of the human community.

4. A recognition that might is not right, that human power is not self-sufficient and absolute.

5. A belief that love, compassion, unselfishness and the force of inner truthfulness and of the spirit ultimately have greater power that hate, enmity and self interest.

6. A sense of obligation to stand on the side of the poor and the oppressed and against the rich and the oppressors.

7. A profound hope that good will finally prevail.

B2: Seven points agreed upon at "Second Parliament of World Religions", Chicago, 1995:

1. We are interdependent. Each of us depends on the well-being of the whole, and so we must have respect for the community of living beings, for people, animals, and plants, and for the preservation of Earth, the air, water and soil.

2. We must take individual responsibility for all we do. All our decisions, actions, and failures to act have consequences.

3. We must treat others as we wish others to treat us. We make a commitment to respect life and dignity, individuality and diversity, so that every person is treated humanely, without exception.

4. We consider humankind to be our family. We must strive to be kind and generous. We must not live for ourselves alone, but should also serve others, never forgetting the children, the aged, the poor, the suffering, the disabled, the refugees and the lonely.

5. We commit ourselves to a culture of non-violence, respect, justice and peace.

6. We must strive for a just social and economic order, in which everyone has an equal chance to reach full potential as a human being. We must move beyond the dominance of greed for power, prestige, money and consumption to make a just and peaceful world.

7. Earth cannot be changed for the better unless the consciousness of individuals is changed first. Therefore we commit ourselves to the global ethic, to understanding one another, and to socially-beneficial, peace-fostering, and nature-friendly ways of life.

APPENDIX C:
PROPOSALS FOR REVISING UN
GENERAL ASSEMBLY VOTING

At present each member nation has one vote in the UN's General Assembly. This means that China, with 1.3 billion people and the United States, with 290 million each have one vote. Iceland and the Maldive Islands each also have one vote, though each has a population of less than 1 million. Differences are even more striking when one considers which countries pay how much to the UN for its operations.

These disparities perhaps have meant little through the years, inasmuch as the General Assembly of the UN has virtually no power. It is a debating body and only makes recommendations to the Security Council. However, in any serious make-over of the UN, a more powerful General Assembly would require a more balanced and fair voting procedure.

C1: Hudson's "Binding Triad" Proposal

In the early 1960s Richard Hudson proposed a modified system of voting in the General Assembly. He called it "The Binding Triad". On any issue requiring a vote each delegate representing a member nation would vote once. But the votes would be calculated in three simultaneous ways. The first count would be is simply a "headcount" of nations for and against the proposal, and 2/3 of the nations must vote "for" a measure for it to be considered for passage. This first calculation has remained the same since Hudson first proposed his triad concept. However he has adjusted his second and third calculations as follows: Nations voting "for" would have to represent over half of the world's population and those same nations would have to account for over half of the monetary contributions made by nations to the UN. On the vote on any measure, if nations voting "for" pass these three calculations, the measure passes, is "binding", and in effect becomes international law. If it fails any of these three "tests", it does not.

Hudson's proposal has been endorsed by organizations and individuals. However, the Binding Triad has yet to be taken up seriously in the UN. Richard Hudson remains very active with the Center for War/Peace Studies and continues to promote his Binding Triad concept.

C2: Schwartzberg's Proposal

A very similar and more recent proposal to modify voting in the UN's General Assembly has been presented by Joseph Schwartzberg. By his proposal each nation's <u>percentage</u> of the world totals of 3 items (1. population, 2. actual financial contributions to the UN, and 3. "percentage of the total UN membership") would be totaled. This total would be the weight of that nation's vote in the General Assembly.

Schwartzberg's three percentages might be simpler to apply than Hudson's in an actual voting situation. Schwartzberg also proposes revisions to the Security Council that would make it more fair and representative of the world's nations and people. (<u>Newsletter: Citizens for Global Solutions of Greater St. Louis</u>, Summer 2004, p. 6.)

APPENDIX D:
UN DIRECT FUNDING OPTIONS

Several options have been proposed through the years by which the UN would have its own direct source of funding for its operational expenses, for peace-keeping and a quick response "Global Peace Force". This would eliminate the UN's dependence on its members paying their specified dues on time, paying "later", or not paying them at all. The United States and perhaps other UN members have opposed this because it would give the UN more power.

Below is a list of at least some of the sources that have been proposed, all of which are in the form of taxes or fees. None of these would compete with revenue sources currently used by nations.

1. The :Tobin Tax", proposed in 1972 by Harvard Professor Tobin, is the best known of these. It is a miniscule tax to be paid to the UN on each international currency transaction. Even a 1/10 of 1% tax would raise about $250 billions a year, far more than the UN's anticipated needs.

2. Harold Stassen proposed a small export/import tax (Appendix E2).

3. A "separation tax", based on tonnage, of materials (mineral ores) removed from the bottom of international waters.

4. A small tax added to each international airline or ocean liner ticket or item of cargo.

5. A very nominal direct but progressive tax on each adult world citizen. Singer's proposal is for a 1% tax on "better-off" world citizens.

6. A global "carbon tax" on fossil fuel use, which would stimulate attention to alternate fuels that would not cause air pollution.

7. A fee for parking a satellite in space.

APPENDIX E:
PROPOSALS FOR MODIFYING
THE UN CHARTER

E1: Key principles of the Clark and Sohn proposal of "The Proposed Revised Charter of the United Nations":

1. A system of enforceable world law must be in effect. Such law must be explicit and apply to nations and individuals.

2. World judicial tribunals must be established and maintained and organs of mediation and conciliation with the end that adjudication and adjustment will replace violence.

3. A permanent global police force of adequate strength must be established and maintained. There must be strong safeguards against its misuse.

4. The complete disarmament of all nations is essential, not just reduction or limitation.

5. To avoid instability and possible conflict, effective world social machinery must be created to deal with the vast disparities in the economic condition of various regions of the world.

6. Virtually all nations must participate in the world organization.

Other revision elements proposed by Clark and Sohn to the UN Charter include: a modified General Assembly that would have power; the Security Council would be replaced by an Executive Council with the veto power eliminated. Clark and Sohn do not propose a direct funding mechanism for the reformed UN; it would still depend on voluntary contributions from member nations.

E2: Main points of Harold Stassen's proposal for restructuring the UN:

1. Revise voting procedure in the General Assembly to include nationhood, population and financial support of the UN and its activities (Hudson's Binding Triad).

2. Enlarge Security Council from 15 to 21 members (but retain the veto).

3. Add new UN units: to deal with the environment; to function as an executive council; to form a UN Legion and Inspection Corps; to form a Panel of Mediators, a Board of Arbitration and a World Court of Equity.

4. Acknowledge UN sovereignty over outer space and sea beds outside national claims.

5. To provide revenue for the modified UN Stassen proposes a half percent export/import tax on goods and objects traded between countries: one-fourth percent to be paid by the exporter, one fourth percent by the importer.

6. The UN to sponsor an annual "Worldwide Conference of Religion".

7. Establish a Research Institute.

E3: H. B. Hollins' 1958 Plan for Reforming the UN:

Although the figures presented in Hollins' analysis and plan are long outdated, a multiplier of about ten would make them relevant to these early years of the twenty-first century.

"A FEW PERTINENT FINANCIAL FACTS AS OF JANUARY 1958"
"(1) Military expenditures of the nations of the world are reliably estimated at *100 billion dollars annually.*
(2) Despite these huge expenditures, the security of all nations is being rapidly reduced to the vanishing point.
(3) The total cost of running the world institutions required for a world system of law including the cost of maintaining a highly trained and well equipped World Police Force of 400,000 men has been estimated at 10 billion dollars annually.
(4) If, from the indicated annual savings of 90 billions, 20 billions were set aside annually for the development of backward areas, making a total of *200 billion dollars in ten years,* there would still remain 70 billions in annual savings to the various governments

to be disposed of by reducing taxes or in whatever way seemed advisable.

(5) The net savings to the United States, after paying its estimated share (one third) of the cost of world institutions and of the development fund, would be about *30 billion dollars annually* based on our current military budget of about 40 billions."

"A SUGGESTED PLAN OF ACTION"
"If a start is to be made toward instituting a world system of law, the following official action seems indicated:

(1) The President should deliver a major foreign policy speech in which he clearly spells out in some detail the *ultimate goal* of our foreign policy in terms of a workable system of world law, indicating the benefits, financial and otherwise, that would accrue to mankind.

(2) The President should announce in the same speech that he was appointing a Commission with instructions to report to him within 18 months exactly what would be required in the way of world institutions if a rule of law were to be established.

(3) The President should urge that the governments of all other nations take similar action with the idea that a United Nations Review Conference would be called within two years."

"A FEW PERTINENT FACTS CONCERNING A U.N. CHARTER REVIEW CONFERENCE"

"(1) A U.N. Charter Review Conference has been voted by the U.N. The date can be set by the General Assembly where no veto applies.

(2) If two-thirds of the delegates at the U.N. Charter Review Conference were to agree to the amendments required to substitute world law for the present competitive armaments system, then the amendments would be recommended by the Conference to the member governments for ratification in accordance with their respective constitutional processes. *There can be no veto at the Review Conference.*

(3) The amendments would take effect when two-thirds of the members of the United Nations including *all* permanent members of the Security Council had ratified them according to their respective constitutional processes."

Hollins, H. B. (Ed), <u>Can America learn about Peace and Freedom from….</u>, NYAD Research, Baltimore, 1958.

Hollins also notes that a failure to ratify at one time does not kill the amendment. It remains fixed and may be ratified later.

APPENDIX F:
WORLD CONSTITUTION DRAFT

Already drafts of several "World Constitutions" have been prepared by legal and other experts. Thus, whenever the human race is ready to consider seriously remodeling the UN or organizing a new Limited World Government organization, these will be useful as "first drafts".

Following are summary concepts from such a draft developed by a group of scholars led by Robert Hutchins, (then) Chancellor of the University of Chicago, in 1948.

Summary concepts of the Hutchins draft of a World Constitution:

a. War must and can be outlawed and peace can and must be universally enacted and enforced;

b. World Government is the only alternative to world destruction;

c. "World Government is necessary, therefore it is possible";

d. The price of World Government and peace is justice.

The Hutchins group proposed a "Federal Republic of the World." Beginning with its dedication to Mahatma Gandhi and a "Declaration of Duties and Rights" of world citizens, it acknowledged that the "the four elements of life— earth, water, air, energy—are the common property of the human race."

The Hutchins group proposed: a Federal Convention made up of delegates elected directly by the people of all nations, the numbers based on population. The Federal Convention to be divided into nine regional "Electoral Colleges" of "kindred nations and cultures". Delegates would vote as individuals, not as representatives of their respective nations or Electoral Colleges, and they would select representatives for the World Council. The World Council would be the legislative body.

Other elements of the Hutchins group proposal were: a President, an executive Chancellor with a Cabinet, a Supreme Court, a Tribune (who would function as spokesperson for minorities), and a Chamber of Guardians (whose duties would be to maintain the peace and direct a military unit).

APPENDIX G:
SOME ORGANIZATIONS AND PUBLICATIONS WITH INFORMATION ON THE UN, WORLD GOVERNMENT, WAR AND MILITARIZATION AND OTHER CRITICAL ISSUES

G1. Organizations.

1. Citizens for Global Solutions, P.O. Box 96222, Washington, D.C., 20090-6222. (also Internet)

2. Internet: <moveon-help@list.moveon.org>

3. Internet: <info@philadelphiaII.us>

4. Internet:

   a. World Constitution and Parliament Assn.

   b. Association to Unite the Democracies.

   c. World Citizens Assembly.

5. "Seeds of Hope", 370 Lexington Ave, New York, NY10017

6. United Nations Association—USA (UNA-USA), 801 Second Ave., New York, NY 10017-4706, also <www.unausa.org>.

7. Center for War/Peace Studies, <Hudson@cwps.org> or 180 West 80th, NY, NY 10024.

G2. Publications.

1. "Amnesty International", Amnesty International USA, 5 Penn Plaza, 14/FL, New York, NY 10001

2. "Church and State", Americans United For Separation of Church and State, 518 C Street NE, Washington, DC 20002

3. "The Defense Monitor", Center for Defense Information, 1779 Massachusetts Ave., NW, Washington, DC 20036

4. "Grass Roots", Ted Braun, Editor, PO Box 330, Pleasant Hill, TN 38578

5. "The Hightower Lowdown", P.O. Box 20596, New York, NY 10011

6. "Intelligence Report" and "Teaching Tolerance", Southern Poverty Law Center, 400 Washington Ave., Montgomery, AL 36104

7. "The Interdependent", published by the UNA-USA (See above)

8. "Liberal Opinion Week", 311 B Ave., Vinton, IA 52349

9. "St. Louis Economic Conversion News", St. Louis Economic Conversion Project, 438 N. Skinker, St. Louis, MO 63130

10. "United World", UNITED WORLD/CDWG NEWS AND VIEWS, Gary K. Shepherd, Editor, 401 S. Dixon, Carbondale, IL 62901

11. "Washington Spectator", PO Box 20065, London Terrace Station, New York, NY 10011

12. "World Watch". Worldwatch Institute, 1776 Massachusetts Ave. NW, Washington, DC 20036

13. "Global Report", Internet

REFERENCES

Note: Several quotes in the text have "Internet" indicated as the source. A few footnoted references are not complete. These items are from my files and include the best information I have.

INTRODUCTION

1. Simon, Paul, <u>Healing America</u>, Orbis Books, Maryknoll, NY, 2003, p. xiv-xv.

2. Huxley, Aldous, <u>Jesting Pilate</u>, New York, Harper, 1928, pp. 322-324.

3. Lyford, Joseph, "Vote for World Peace", <u>New Republic</u>, 12-27-48), pp. 16-18.

4. Cousins, Norman, editorial: "The Number-One Problem", <u>Saturday Review</u>, Mar. 15, 1980, p. 10.

5. Hollins, Harry B (Ed.), <u>Can America learn about Peace and Freedom from…</u>, NYAD Research, Baltimore, 1958, p. 20.

6. Ibid.

PART I—OUR TROUBLED WORLD

1. Zinn, Howard, <u>You Can't Be Neutral on a Moving Train</u>, Beacon Press, Boston, 1994–2001, p.8.

A. OUR WORLD OF EXTREMES

2. Pearson, Lester, "The Four Faces of Peace", reprinted by Sidney Hillman Foundation, Inc.

3. Ward, Barbara, and Rene Dubos, <u>Only One Earth</u>, W. W. Norton, New York, 1972, p. 218.

4. Presidential Commission on World Hunger, 1979 Report, p. I.3.

5. Scott, Bruce, "The Great Divide in the Global Village", Foreign Affairs, Jan–Feb 2001, p. 174.

6. Landers, Ann, "Summary of the World", Southern Illinoisan, 6-2-97.

PART II—THREE KEY PROBLEMS

A. GOVERNMENT AND WAR

1. Wells, H. G., Guide to the New World, Gollanz, London, 1941, p. 66.

2. Zinn, op. cit., pp. 98-99.

3. Warburg, James P., The West in Crisis, Doubleday, Garden City, 1959, pp. 162-4, 166-7.

4. Bush, George Herbert Walker, Internet.

5. Clinton, Bill, Internet.

6. Schmookler, Andrew Bard, The Parable of the Tribes, Houghton Mifflin, New York, 1984, p. 54.

7. Ibid., p. 35.

8. Simon, Paul, "Choosing Wisely in Matters of War: Some Lessons from History", "P.S./Washington" (Paul's weekly column), May 12-18, 1991.

9. Simon, Paul, "The Iraqi Crisis: Legal and Socio-Economic Dimensions", Southern Illinois University Law Journal, Spring 1991, pp. 411-412.

10. Simon, Healing America, op. cit., p. 116.

11. Eisenhower, op. cit., Radio and TV address and Internet.

12. Benjamin C., New Legal Foundations for Global Survival, (ISBN 0-379-21207-2, ca 1994), p. 199.

13. Denny, Jeffrey, "Who Needs Enemies?", Common Cause Magazine, Fall 1992, p. 30.

14. Reves, Emery, The Anatomy of Peace, Pocket Books, New York, 1946, p. 37-38.

15. Einstein, Internet, "The Wit and Wisdom of Albert Einstein".

16. Hollins, Henry B., Powers & Sommer, The Conquest of War, Westview Press, Boulder, CO, 1989, pp. 1-2.

B. GLOBALIZATION AND MAKING A LIVING

17. Wilson, Woodrow, Internet.

18. "Norway Tops UN Ranking", <u>News of Norway</u>, August 2004.

19. Roosevelt, Franklin, Internet.

20. Stites, Tom, "How Corporations Became Persons'", <u>Unitarian-Universalist World</u>, May-June 2003. Also: The Hightower Lowdown, April 2003.

21. Mekay, Emad, Internet, Inter Press Service, Friday, April 23, 2004.

22. Simon, op. cit., p. 66.

C. THE EARTH AND PEOPLE

23. Marsh, George, <u>The Earth As Modified by Human Action</u>, Charles Scribner & Sons, New York, 1874.

24. Lowdermilk, W. C., "Conquest of the Land Through Seven Thousand Years", U.S. Department of Agriculture, Soil Conservation Service document SCS-MP, Feb. 1948, mimeographed, and Agric. Info. Bulletin 99, US-GPO, Aug. 1953.

25. Vogt, William, <u>Road to Survival</u>, William Sloan, New York, 1948, p. ix.

26. "United Nations warns world's land turning to desert at alarming speed", <u>The Southern Illinoisan</u>, June 16, 2004, p. 8D.

27. Simon, op. cit. p. 146.

28. Carter, Vernon Gill, <u>Man on the Landscape</u>, National Wildlife Federation, Washington, D.C., 1949, pp. 2-3.

29. Brown, Lester, <u>Plan B: Rescuing a Planet Under Stress and a Civilization in Trouble</u>, W. W. Norton & Co., New York, 2003.

30. Udall, Stewart, "Let's Stop Sleepwalking Through History", <u>Liberal Opinion Week,</u> December 27, 2004, p. 8.

31. Toffler, Alvin, <u>The Third Wave</u>, William Morrow, NY, 1980, pp. 210-224, 355-6, etc.

32. Kennedy, Robert F., Jr., <u>Crimes Against Nature</u>, Harper Collins, London, pp. 4-5.

33. Cousins, Norman, Internet.

34. Simon, op. cit., p. 37.

PART III—HUMAN MADE PROBLEMS MUST BE SOLV ED BY HUMANS

1. Douglas, William O., 1952

2. Gore, Alvin, <u>The Earth in Balance</u>, Plume/Penguin, NY, 1993, p. 301.

3. Schopenhauer, Andrew, Internet.

A. STRUGGLES TOWARD WORLD PEACE

4. Curtis, Lionel, <u>World Order</u>, Oxford University, NY, 1939.

5. Wynner, Edith and Georgia Lloyd, <u>Searchlight on Peace Plans: Choose Your Road to World Government</u>, E. P. Dutton, New York, 1949.

6. Cleveland, Harlan, <u>The Third Try at World Order</u>, Aspen Institute for Humanistic Studies, New York, 1976.

7. Davis, Garry, <u>World Government Ready of Not!</u>, Juniper Ledge Publishing Co., Sorrento, ME, 1984.

8. Hudgens, Thomas A., <u>Let's.Abolish.War.</u>, BILR Corp., Denver, 1986, p. 86.

9. Cousins, Norman, Internet.

10. Eisenhower, Dwight, <u>Crusade in Europe</u>, Doubleday, 1948.

B. FERMENT TOWARD "PEACE ON EARTH"

11. Reves, op. cit., 37-8.

12. Lyford, op. cit.

13. Glossop, <u>World Federation? A critical Analysis of Federal World Government</u>, McFarland, Jefferson, NC, 1993, p. 178.

14. Wallace, Henry, <u>Toward World Peace</u>, Reynal & Hitchcock, NYC, 1948, p. 109.

15. Vonnegut, Kurt, "Cold Turkey", <u>Alternet</u> on the Internet, June 7, 2004.

C. EDUCATION, HEALTH CARE AND PEACE

16. Higbee, Edward, <u>The Squeeze: Cities Without Space</u>, William Morrow, New York, 1960, p. 280.

D. CHARACTERISTICS OF A VIABLE LIMITED WORLD GOVERNMENT

17. Hollins, et al, op. cit., pp. 78-88.

18. Andrews, Paul S., "Neutrals for Peace", World Assembly of World Federalists, The Hague, Netherlands, 1962.

E. HOW TO ACHIEVE LIMITED WORLD GOVERNMENT

19. Hollins, et al, op. cit., pp. 38-53.

20. Rosenfeld, George, The Catalyst, Rosenfeld Publishing, Berea, OH, 1982.

21. Ferencz, op. cit., p. 260 and Chap. 8.

22. Stassen, Harold, A Working Paper for Restructuring the United Nations, Lerner Publications, Minneapolis, 1994.

23. Ferencz, op. cit., p. 381.

F. OPPOSITION TO LIMITED WORLD GOVERNMENT

24. Friedman, Thomas, The World Is Flat, Farrar, Straus and Giroux, New York, 2005.

25. Bower, Bruce, "Buyers Beware", Science News, 9-6-03.

26. Glossop, op. cit., pp. 133-4.

27. Reves, op. cit., p. 69.

G. NINETEEN HOPEFUL SIGNS

28. Ivins, Molly, "Bum Rap", Southern Illinoisan, 12-8-99.

PART IV—URGENCY AND CHALLENGE

1. Curtis, Lionel, op. cit., p. 910.

2. World Bank, "1994 Human Development Report".

3. Pitts, Leonard, "New children's book on slavery puts black history in proper light", The Southern Illinoisan, December 29, 2004.

4. Reves, op. cit., p. 83.

5. Mallaby, Sebastian, "The Reluctant Imperialist: Terrorism, Failed States, and the Case for American Empire", Foreign Affairs, Mar.-Apr. 2002.

A. A WEB OF SURVIVAL

B. WHAT CAN WE DO?

   6. Reves, <u>A Democratic Manifesto</u>, Random House, New York, 1942, p. 143.

C. THE ATHENIANS

   7. Gibbon, Edward, Internet.

   8. da Silva, Luiz Inacio Lula, at June 2004 meeting of the UN Conference on Trade and Development.

   9. Singer, Peter, <u>One World, the Ethics of Globalization</u>, Yale University Press, New Haven & London, 2002, p. 7.

10. Ibid., p. 194.

11. Simon, Paul, <u>Healing America</u>, op. cit., p. 92.

12. Ibid., p. 63.

13. Ibid., p. 138.

D. CONCLUSION

14. Gore, op cit., pp. 295-360.

15. Brzezinski, Zbigniew, <u>The Choice</u>, Perseus Books, NY, 2004, pp. viii-x.

16. Simon, op. cit., p. xv.

17. Ibid., p. 153.

18. Hollins (Ed.), op. cit., p. 20.

19. Ibid.

20. Simon, op. cit., p. 161.

EPILOGUE

   1. Schopenhauer, A, Internet.

   2. Cronkite, W, Address to the UN, October 1999, Internet.

   3. Johnson, L, Address to the UN, December 1963, Internet.

   4. Eisenhower, D, Address to American People, October 31, 1956, Internet.

INDEX

978-0-595-36386-5
0-595-36386-5

www.ingramcontent.com/pod-product-compliance
Lightning Source LLC
Chambersburg PA
CBHW022247290526
45785CB00015B/390